Marriage Equality USA

VISION AND MISSION

We believe in a world that protects and celebrates
families without regard to sexual orientation or gender
identity. Our mission is to secure legally recognized
civil marriage equality for LGBTQ families at the
state and federal level through grassroots organizing,
education, action, and partnerships.

The People's Victory

STORIES FROM THE FRONT LINES IN THE
FIGHT FOR MARRIAGE EQUALITY

Copyright © 2017 by Marriage Equality USA

Published by Marriage Equality USA
P.O. Box 121
Old Chelsea Station
New York, NY 10113

ISBN 9781495639074 *June*

Designed in San Francisco, CA by Brian Cox at
Brian Cox Design.

Typeset in Filosofia (designed by Zuzana Licko)
and Meta (designed by Erik Spiekermann).

Printed and bound in Chicago, IL by Edward
Brothers Malloy.

Distributed by INscribe Digital.

Edited by Christine Allen, Judi Berzon, Kirsten
Berzon, Zack Lyons, Alex May, Christopher
Michaud, Liz Noteware, and Brian Silva. ∞

The People's Victory

STORIES FROM THE FRONT LINES IN THE
FIGHT FOR MARRIAGE EQUALITY

MARRIAGE EQUALITY USA, *publisher*

Contents

Foreword

— LIEUTENANT GOVERNOR GAVIN NEWSOM

The story of marriage equality is often told as a series of major events. The big court case. The nail-biting vote. The politician taking a stand.

The truth is that as important as those are, the real road to victory was paved with the unsung, everyday deeds of hundreds of thousands of brave, ordinary individuals. Grandparents. Siblings. Friends. Coworkers. Neighbors. Those who created the conditions that enabled millions of honest conversations to take root around family breakfast tables nationwide, breaking the silence on the unmentionable. These individuals, many who found training, support and a home for their activism in Marriage Equality USA (MEUSA), were the backbone of changing the hearts and minds of a nation that had told them their love, commitment, and families were not good enough to be recognized.

I was fortunate enough to have seen first hand a few of the stories and events recounted in *The People's Victory*. From the marriages we performed at City Hall during 2004's "Winter of Love," to watching the justices of the U.S. Supreme Court, these events reminded me how profoundly LGBTQ people deserved the right to marry the person they loved.

Throughout those years, the grassroots volunteers in MEUSA and elsewhere showed us that no change worth its salt happens on its own. It takes organization and working slowly, one person at a time, to build momentum and a critical mass for change. The grassroots movement's success was in listening, teaching, and trusting individuals and local communities to do what was right for them. They faced defeat and loss head on, learning it was often two steps forward and one step (or even two or three) back before success was achieved.

The People's Victory is a mirror for each of us to see our own power to fight for justice and create the change we want to see in our world. Marriage equality was the vehicle for these authors – but what will yours be? I hope these stories inspire you to resist, to fight, to win, and in the end write the next stories in our continuing push for a more just and perfect union.

Introduction

— BRIAN SILVA

The story of marriage equality is the story of you.

In creating *The People's Victory*, we wanted to show the world the power of everyday individuals to bring about monumental change. The blockbuster and headline grabbing moments have (rightfully) been covered in books, television, and even film. But as a grassroots organization, Marriage Equality USA (MEUSA) has always believed this fight for hearts and minds was something only achievable when everyday people not only believed they had the power to make change, but acted on it. In fact, millions of you did.

Some, like Edie Windsor, took a small action at a Marriage Equality New York (MENY) meeting that eventually helped lead her to become a household name with a winning case at the United States Supreme Court. Others, like Leslie Stewart, balanced out a local news story by being the only pro-marriage sign at an opposition event. At the heart of these, and all of the stories contained in this book, is that each author made the choice to act! Taking action is the crucial part of any social justice movement. We can no longer assume or hope others will stand up and act for what is right; we have to be those people.

While the vehicle for this social justice journey was marriage equality, our vision for this book is for readers to find inspiration, power, and the will to work for whatever social justice issue they are passionate about: from women's rights and the environment, to racial and economic justice. The fight to be treated equally in marriage cannot end at the altar or county clerk's office. Those forces seeking to deny same-sex couples equal marriage rights for so long are the same people, ideologies and resources working against anyone who is pushing our country to be more fair and just.

The People's Victory elevates and honors the everyday heroes of social justice who make the brave decision to no longer sit idly on the sidelines of history. Instead, they hold a sign, attend a meeting, and share their stories. They are you.

1998 **1999** **2000** **2004** **2005**

Februray 12
Founded
Begun as a Equality Through Marriage on National Freedom to Marry Day and became Marriage Equality New York (MENY) that August.

Marriage Equality 101
Created first public education workshops for groups, lawmakers, etc. on why marriage mattered.

MECA
Inspired and assisted by MENY, California activists found Marriage Equality Californina (MECA).

Marriage Counter Actions
Started by other California activisits, same-sex couples request marriage licenses to give a public face to their inequality and hurt.

Get Engaged Tours
Annual talks, especially in rural and conservative areas, to engage the public in the fight.

Bridge Walks (aka The Wedding March)
Begun by MENY in New York City, thousands marched across California and New York bridges to symbolize crossing the "bridge" to equality.

October 11
National Marriage Rally
First national rally. Held in Washington D.C. at the end of the Marriage Equality Express.

October
Marriage Equality Express
Bus caravan from California to Washington D.C. in response to the voiding of 4,000+ California marriages. Held education events in towns across the country.

Tax Day Actions
Volunteers at post offices on Tax Day give leaflets about financial and tax inequalities when you can't marry.

2006　2007　2011　2012　2013/2015　2016

MEUSA Founded
After a failed merger, former MECA volunteers start Marriage Equality USA (MEUSA, a national grassroots group.

The Loving Quilt
National touring quilt, each family panel had stories and pictures to honor San Francisco same-sex weddings and Loving v. Virginia decision.

Walk a Mile in My Shoes
Public art at New York capital building of stories, with shoes attached, of those hurt by a lack of marriage equality. After, shoes and stories were regularly sent to legislators as reminders.

Online Resource Center
One of the first complete sites for tracking legislation, polling, and court cases.

National Equality Action Team (NEAT)
A MEUSA-led coalition to let volunteers everywhere phone bank and canvass for marriage campaigns anywhere.

New York Win and Merger
After MENY co-led win in New York, they merged with MEUSA to win nationwide.

Unite for Marriage
Co-led rallies at Supreme Court and supported hundreds of local events during arguments and decisions.

20th Anniversa
Announced decision to suns with a series of celebrations nationwide and an archive and book project.

The Walls, Did Indeed, Talk

— CHRISTINE ALLEN

Pine trees and rivers remind me of Nevada County in the Sierra Foothills of Northern California. This is where I lived when I first became active in the American marriage equality movement. During February 2005 Marriage Equality California (MECA) activists were hitting the roads for their annual "Get Engaged Tour," and as a result of this tour I stepped into the whirlwind atmosphere of the movement's front lines as the Nevada County Chapter Leader for MECA.

In the late spring of 2005, the core members of our Nevada County Chapter gathered at a local Unitarian Universalist church to train for an upcoming day of canvassing in support of CA Assemblyperson Mark Leno's AB 849.[1] Our trainer spent the afternoon teaching people who hadn't done this before how to "cut turf," and had them role play talking to the public about the issue of marriage equality and why we would like them to contact their legislators and urge them to vote in support of passing AB 849.

We snacked on cookies and fresh veggies, sipped coffee, water, and tea throughout the warm afternoon. I appreciated the folks who had turned out, as well as the young trainer's enthusiasm and ability to clarify the time-worn campaign tool of cutting turf. Dust motes floated through the air in the light streaming in from a stained window. The event was informal and intimate, in the way working for a shared cause can be.

One of the things we discussed at length was the social and political conservatism of the majority of our county's residents. Although the county was diverse class-wise and politically, the Republicans still held a clear majority in this overwhelmingly white semi-rural area. One of the places we would

14

be canvassing was a mobile home park for seniors, and several of the people present were concerned about the reception we would receive there. Would this be a day of doors slammed in our faces or would we have the opportunity to actually engage and talk with people?

Our canvassing day dawned clear and hot. Gorgeous, but not the most comfortable for a day of walking door-to-door. The spirits of our small group seemed to be energetic and hopeful, which I found to be encouraging. At least our people weren't put off by their concerns, or cynicism in some cases, regarding our possible reception. After settling on times and a location to touch base with each other during the day, we split into pairs and headed off in different directions.

Thankfully, Nevada County is full of trees, even in town, so as the hours passed and we began to tire and wear down from thirst and the heat, there was usually somewhere on each block to catch a few moments in the shade. My buddy Steve and I eventually entered the mobile home park for seniors, each of us working one side of each block. At many houses nobody came to the door, even though it appeared someone was home. Other doors opened, but the people were curt and shut the door quickly after answering it. Every so often someone would politely hear us out, which gave us just enough encouragement to continue.

Late in the afternoon, I approached a neat white home fronted by flowers and ringed by pine trees in back. I was thankful that the front porch was shaded. After my knock the door was opened by an elderly woman, tall and slim, white hair permed and blued, dressed in a casual "duster," but holding herself with dignity. She greeted me courteously and I eased into my spiel. She listened carefully, and then announced that I needed to know she was a lifelong Republican who always voted. "And, you know where my party stands on this issue, don't you?" Yes, I did. She hesitated and then began to tell me about a movie she had seen on TV. The movie was *If These Walls Could Talk 2.*[2]

She asked me if I was familiar with it, and I told her I was. She got a faraway look in her eyes and began to relay one of the scenes in the movie. In this scene, an older lesbian widow is sitting on a living room chair watching as her newly deceased partner's nephew and his wife go through her home, casually picking up and taking or tossing aside treasured items the lesbian couple had collected in their years together. As they do this, the man is telling the widow that he had considered allowing her to continue to live in the house as a rental tenant, but had decided to sell the property and that she would have to move. The widow, sitting in her home of decades, having just lost her love to an unexpected death, is being treated as a total stranger with no claim to her home and with absolutely no acknowledgment of her loss and the grief she is experiencing. It is a wrenching, emotionally powerful scene.

As she told me the story, the woman's eyes filled with tears and she brokenly tried to explain to me how that story, and that particular scene, had affected her. She whispered, "Nobody should have to go through that. Nobody!" Then she wiped at the tears on her face and firmly told me that she would, indeed, call her assemblyperson and senator and urge them both to vote in favor of AB 849. She patted my arm, and murmured, "Good luck, dear. I need to go lie down now."

I stumbled down the steps with tears in my own eyes. This one conversation made that hot day of canvassing worthwhile. This one conversation made all of our efforts in support of this particular marriage equality bill worthwhile. In fact, the memory of this one conversation sustained me through many low points during the ensuing decade of my work for marriage equality.

That dignified woman under the pines on that hot day in Nevada County, she embodied the changing of "hearts and minds" to me. She still does. ∞

—

1 Bill AB 19, the "Religious Freedom and Civil Marriage Protection Act," authored by then California Assemblyperson Mark Leno, was passed by the CA Assembly's Judiciary and Appropriations Committees. However, the bill died on 2 June 2005, after failing to obtain a majority. The bill would have extended marriage to same-sex couples in California. AB 19 was later reactivated and introduced by Assembly person Leno as AB 849. In September 2005 AB 849 was passed by the full CA legislature – historically, this was the first piece of marriage equality legislation in the country to be passed by a statehouse, but the bill was vetoed by then Governor Arnold Schwarzenegger later that same month.

2 If These Walls Could Talk 2 is a 2000 television movie in the United States, broadcast on HBO. It follows three separate storylines about lesbian couples in three different time periods. As with the original If These Walls Could Talk, all the stories are set in the same house across different time periods.

MENY's "Say 'I Do' Tour"

— FRED ANGUERA

In May of 2011, before the passage of marriage equality in New York State, Ron Zacchi, the then executive director of MENY (Marriage Equality New York), and I went on a month-long walking and biking tour around the state. We were rallying and generating press for the cause. It was called the "Say 'I Do' Tour." During the tour, Ron and I walked over 220 miles and biked about 400 miles.

Halfway through the tour, during the walking part before we began biking, we were finishing the last part of the walk from Buffalo to Rochester, and we were feeling pretty beaten up, especially me with an injured left ankle. We stayed overnight at a volunteer's house somewhere between Buffalo and Rochester; someone who was kind enough to put us up at his home for free. He left for work early the next morning and told us to just lock the door behind us when we left.

There was a sweet dog that lived there named Roberta. As we were leaving, Roberta decided she also wanted to leave, to stretch her legs around town. Although Roberta was an older dog, she could still run! The more I approached her to get her back to the house, the more she ran. When I realized that Roberta had no intention of coming back to the house, I yelled to Ron, "Do NOT close and lock the door," and, with my swollen ankle, I proceeded to chase Roberta around the town, screaming, "ROBERTA, ROBERTA, GET BACK HERE YOU NAUGHTY DOG!!!" I felt horrible and thought to myself, here this kind family opened their home to us, trusted us, and now I was going to lose their dog. What a thing to happen on the last day of our long walk!

After about 20 minutes, I could tell Roberta was becoming worn out. Her age was finally catching up with her and I was able to match her pace. With my

17

ankle throbbing, and sweat dripping off me, I finally was able to grab her collar while in mid-run, stop her, and bring her back to the house. Sweet relief!

During our 30-mile walk that day – which we started way later than we had intended to – I had a lot of time to reflect. While I limped along to Rochester, I couldn't help but think that my mad dash that morning to catch Roberta and get her back to the house was much like the quest for marriage equality in the State of New York. It hurt, it was messy, it seemed like it was taking forever, we were so close and yet it kept slipping away. We really needed to "catch" marriage equality and to bring the issue of equal rights back to the house of justice where it belonged! My painful, swollen, left ankle and I were happy to get on a bike the next day as Ron and I continued our tour on to Syracuse, Utica, and eventually, down to Long Island.

The very next month marriage equality passed in New York State! And, the "Say 'I Do' Tour" had passed through the districts of all four Republican Senators who voted in favor of the NY Marriage Equality Bill. Just like Roberta, equality had been successfully returned to the house of justice. ∞

—

Fred is also the producer of a visual history of MENY called *History in the Making: A Grassroots Fight for Marriage Equality*, which can be found at https://vimeo.com/226529063 using password 'equality.'

Live Your Life Out Loud —
You Can Change the World

— SHELLY BAILES

It's hard for me to say why my life took the path it did. When I was a kid grow-ing up I had lots of friends and always felt that it was important to stand up for what I thought was right. When my public school in NY decided that girls were not allowed to wear pants to school, I protested and was made to sit out in the hall the whole day. I remember winning that fight and girls were once again allowed to dress how they wanted. In my life, I can remember standing up and speaking out for so many things, and never feeling ashamed or embarrassed.

Then one day, I fell for one of my girlfriends. I knew this was something that would not go over big if anyone found out about it. Suddenly, I felt ashamed and embarrassed, a feeling I would hide for a very long time. I was told that I should get married, have two kids, and live happily ever after. So, I got married and had two kids. I was not a happy camper. I played the little housewife and tried to make the marriage work. I became president of the local Civic Association and fought to keep our neighborhood safe and clean. I was also president of the PTA. I still wasn't a happy camper.

One day, I discovered a gay bar and my life changed. I met people that felt like I did and I made some wonderful friends. One of these friends introduced me to Ellen. My life changed forever that day.

Ellen and I moved in together in June 1974. Being gay was not easy in the '70s. When we met we were both in the midst of getting divorced. Both of our lawyers told us that our kids would be taken away from us if anyone found out about our relationship. Since Ellen's ex-husband was not fit to take care of her two kids at that time, they would be put into foster care if that happened. We had to call the police when Ellen's ex-husband cut the phone wires and kicked

top–bottom

Ellen and Shelly.

Shelly and Ellen, at
the moment they we
pronounced married

19

in our front door. The police came and sided with him because they said they didn't get involved in domestic affairs. When I complained, they told me that I had no right living there. I once again felt embarrassed and ashamed. It was scary. I remember thinking, "We have to keep this quiet." No more fighting for what's right … there's too much at stake.

We took our kids and moved to Northern California a couple years later and continued to keep quiet. But then something happened. In 1978 we went to San Francisco's Gay Pride Day and Harvey Milk was on stage. He said that the most important thing one could do for the movement was to come out. I decided that I had to do that. I had to be visible and come out. I felt it was the right thing to do. I had to stop being ashamed or embarrassed.

Twenty-two years later, we met Molly McKay who was looking for people to join a relatively new organization called MECA (Marriage Equality California). After talking with her, we knew that this was a fight we had to get involved in. So, we became marriage equality advocates and MECA chapter leaders for our county.

We protested at the post office every Tax Day. We went to county clerks' offices on Valentine's Day and tried to get a marriage license. We kissed in front of the anti-gay protesters. Our faces were in all the major newspapers, in the U.S. and beyond. It was a fight that lasted many years, but I was happy. I wasn't embarrassed or ashamed. I was a happy camper. We were slowly changing the hearts and minds of thinking and caring people. In 2008, we fought hard and lost our battle against Prop 8 which took away marriage rights for same-sex couples in California.

We were heartbroken when Prop 8 passed, but looking back it was one of the best things that could have happened. That event opened up so many minds; minds that will never be closed again. The one conversation that touched me the most is the day we were at a social event and a man I didn't remember ever meeting before asked if he could sit with my wife and me at our table. He started the conversation by telling us that we had met before while working on behalf of a candidate running for our local City Council. He told us that he had voted "Yes" on Prop 8. I thought to myself, "Oh no, here it comes." Then he explained that seeing us during the campaign he noticed that how we treated each other and how we worked together was no different than the way he and his wife interacted. This realization changed him profoundly. He became a supporter of gay rights and said he would never vote against gay rights again. We've since become friends. He made me realize that we'd done the job we set out to do.

Ellen and I got married the first second it was legal, on June 16, 2008 at 5:01 p.m. (five months before Prop 8 passed). I always said that I wanted to be married to Ellen for as long as I could. We have now been together for 42 years and legally married for almost 8 years. I am a happy camper. ∞

Live Your Life Out Loud — You Can Change the World

SHELLY BAILES

Defining Marriage:
Voices from a Forty-Year Labor of Love

— MATT BAUME

The following is adapted from Matt Baume's book, "Defining Marriage: Voices from a Forty-Year Labor of Love."

I spent the morning of March 27, 2013 sitting in the back row of the U.S. Supreme Court, surrounded by governmental opulence, peering at the Justices between gigantic red velvet curtains draped between marble columns.

It was the second day of oral argument concerning gay marriage, and I had been able to finagle a ticket that would allow me a five-minute glimpse at the proceedings. I felt a bit like Forrest Gump to be perched at that particular crossroads of history – a nobody-special who just happened to be watching the world change from an accidental front-row seat.

As the sun rose, the crowd of protesters swelled, waving banners and chanting slogans with their frosty breath in the spring morning air. Milling around, I spotted MEUSA Co-President Cathy Marino-Thomas in the crowd. We had only ever communicated via video-conference from across the country, and there was something perfect about meeting in-person here, at the country's fulcrum of justice. "Hey!" I waved, delighted.

Cathy warmly patted me on the shoulder. "This is it," she smiled, gazing up at the court. Around us milled hundreds of people bearing rainbows and American flags, edging right up to the stairs before security guards chased them back down. They were here thanks to the partnership of groups like MEUSA, which mobilized countless supporters across the country, and various other nonprofits.

Handmade rainbow signs and pink lettering fluttered above us. There was

22

a college-age kid with crude whiskers painted on his face and a sign reading "Cats 4 equality." I love this image. Multiple protesters waved signs about equality for Dumbledore. At the front of the procession, a man in a pink mesh bodysuit, rainbow tutu, and devil horns twirled around, giving "respectable gays" heart palpitations.

The Justices didn't see any of this, of course. They were ensconced deep in their stone chamber, high on the hill behind the raucous crowd. When I entered on the second day of oral argument, all I could manage to whisper was "wow." A security guard 30 feet away shushed me.

"What gives the federal government the right to be concerned at all at what the definition of marriage is?" Justice Sotomayor asked at the front of the courtroom. The hearing had been under way for some time before I was able to enter.

"You know, the federal government recognizes that it's a big player in the world," said attorney Paul Clement after some back-and-forth. He was the attorney representing a group of Republicans who saw political capital in the tormenting of gay couples. "It has a lot of programs that might give states incentives to change the rules one way or another."

Clement was arguing in favor of DOMA, the 1996 law that prevented same-sex married couples from being recognized as "spouses" for the purpose of federal laws. Clement's justification for the law was that the federal government simply wanted to maintain marriage as a system of incentives for stable relationships, but Justice Ginsburg was skeptical of Clement's argument. While he stuttered about "additional benefits," Ginsburg interrupted: "You're saying, no, state, that there are two kinds of marriages. The full marriage, and then this sort of," she searched for the right term, "skim milk marriage."

The audience giggled at that, and Clement bristled. "The federal government has the authority to define the terms that appear in their own statute," he told the court. "In those areas, they are going to have their own definition."

There it was: definition. Who gets to define marriage? Thanks to some disapproving legislators in 1996, the federal government had a narrow definition, limited only to straight couples. In 2013, nine states had a definition that included gay and lesbian couples. And as for me – well, I wasn't sure what my definition was. That's why I wanted to see the papers of Frank Kameny, a pre-Harvey Milk activist. I knew that Frank had left his papers to the Library of Congress. And as one of the twentieth century's foremost architects of gay liberation, I was curious if there was anything in his writings about marriage.

Hidden amongst the folders I was given was a typewritten press release on green carbon paper, clearly an early draft with corrections scribbled in red ink. "TWO HOMOSEXUAL MEN TO APPLY FOR D. C. MARRIAGE LICENSE" it blared. "On Monday, July 3, 1972, Mr. Arthur G. MacDonald, aged 22, and Mr. Frank M. Magill, aged 21, will apply for a license to be married in the District of Columbia."

But there was no indication of what happened to Arthur and Frank. Then, a few pages later, I found an invitation from another gay couple, signed "John and Wayne," followed by the program from their wedding. Or was it a wedding? Were they married? They never used those words, I realized. "CELEBRATION OF THE HOLY UNION," it said at the top of the program.

Then I found a 1978 invitation to a party for William and Aubrey "in celebration of the fifth anniversary of their Holy Union" at a townhouse a few blocks from the National Mall.

After that: Allan and Larry's "Holy Union in Christ" on July 18, 1980. That was one month before I was born.

Michelle and Louise requested "the honor of your presences as they commit themselves to each other before God in a service of Holy Union." Folded in my hands were the artifacts left by couples who, decades earlier, had taken up the rites of marriage and made them their own. Did Arthur and Frank love each other? How did Michelle and Louise decide that the time was right to ... well, what? To marry? To Holy-Unionize? Why didn't any of them use the word "marriage"?

Even after the marriage protesters and the Supreme Court Justices dispersed for the day, the debate certainly wasn't resolved. I thought back to the brief snippet I'd heard of DOMA-defender Paul Clement's position, that marriage is just a system of benefits wielded by a bureaucracy, a system of incentives and rules. Okay, I thought, having hospital visitation and tax bene-

24

fits are nice, but it's not a particularly romantic reason to wed.

Then there was Justice Ginsburg's understanding of the status quo: "full marriage, and then this sort of skim milk marriage." That's the best that most same-sex couples could look forward to at the time: Thin, watered-down, not quite suitable for baking a wedding cake. But then what about those 1970's couples? They had no access to paperwork of any kind. No civil unions, no benefits, no skim milk. They had nothing – or did they?

What they had were love and commitment. They had ceremonies; they had family and friends. They apparently considered themselves joined in, if not marriage, then something close to it. They had the bravery to do so.

As impossible as it must have seemed to them that they would ever find acceptance, they didn't wait for permission to change the world. And decades later, there in Washington D.C., neither did we. ∞

Ding Dong Prop 8 Is Dead

— KIRSTEN BERZON

Déjà vu. Another early morning armed with my cup of coffee and the refresh button. The SCOTUS blog had become a source of potential elation or heartache over those long weeks in June 2013. You might not know what SCOTUS is. I didn't either. It's the acronym for the Supreme Court of the United States, AKA the nine people who would either uphold my second class citizenship or grant me equal justice under the law. All of the marriage equality advocates I knew were experiencing the same emotional roller coaster that June.

On Wednesday, June 26, 2013, the wait was finally over. The Supreme Court of the United States declined to decide the Prop 8 case based on standing, effectively bringing marriage equality back to California. In the Defense of Marriage Act case, the court granted federal marriage benefits to those who already enjoyed the state benefits of marriage, if they were lucky enough to live in marriage equality states.

The second I saw the decisions come across my computer screen, I burst into tears. I think I cried for at least five minutes. Exclamations of "LOVE WON" lit up my Facebook wall. After fighting for marriage equality with Marriage Equality USA for the past seven years, I once again lived in an equality state and my wife and I would also enjoy the 1,183 federal benefits of marriage. While we hoped for this incredible victory, we had experienced many defeats over the years and had learned not to be too optimistic, too soon. The pain of Prop 8's passage and its aftermath was very real. And now, nearly five years later, the relief was palpable.

There was no time to take it in though. We had an event to plan! With several "this could be the day" behind us, today was actually what was dubbed

26

by marriage equality advocates nationwide as the Day of Decision. A small group of Bay Area Marriage Equality USA volunteers, longtime LGBT activists, LGBT community members, and straight allies had been planning Day of Decision for weeks. I use the word "planning" somewhat loosely because how can you plan an event for tens of thousands of people in San Francisco's Castro District without knowing when it will be? But somehow, we did it!

As soon as we heard the news early that Wednesday morning, we went into action. We had to rent the truck which would serve as our event stage. There was extensive coordination with the San Francisco Police Department regarding street closures, blockades, and parking. We had to activate the evening's speakers who had been on standby for weeks and tell them that today was the day. We had to get the word out so people would come to Castro and Market that evening for the celebration. The "to do" list was long, but our small but mighty crew was ready to tackle it.

Even though we already had designated media spokespeople, some of us went through training so multiple members of the team could respond to the media onslaught. Others put up "No Parking" signs on meters up and down Castro Street. Yet others talked with local businesses so they would be prepared for thousands of celebrants who would descend upon the neighborhood that evening. The feeling of unbridled joy that afternoon in the Castro is still something I remember vividly to this day. There was freedom in the air as strangers hugged, horns honked, and rainbow flags waved.

The San Francisco 2013 Day of Decision event drew an estimated 30,000 people, packed into a very few blocks along Castro Street and the surrounding side streets. Two stages. Dozens of speakers. Live music performances. Clergy from the Coalition of Welcoming Congregations. Pioneers in the LGBT civil rights movement. They were all there. Standing on the stage, looking down Castro Street at the jubilant crowd, I was overwhelmed and incredibly proud. Our little ragtag group of dedicated volunteers had made this happen.

When I think about that day, as well as my tenure as a marriage equality activist, I keep coming back to the famous quote by Margaret Mead: "Never doubt that a small group of thoughtful, committed citizens can change the world; indeed, it's the only thing that ever has." As we continue to strive toward a day when every LGBT person not only enjoys the benefits of marriage, but also the joy of full lived equality in all aspects of their lives, I will always be proud of the powerful community of Marriage Equality USA Love Warriors with whom I worked over the years. ∞

Ding Dong
Prop 8 Is Dead

KIRSTEN BERZON

28

The Long Wait Is Over

— MICHAEL BOYAJIAN

In 2005 I had been working with the Freemasons and a New York City hospital on setting up a summer camp for HIV teens. I found a camp, but the hospital dropped the project. Soon after that my Freemason friend Dave Warren called and told me to call Cathy Marino-Thomas, the chair of Marriage Equality New York (MENY), and help her out.

I called Cathy and she told me the LGBT community wanted marriage rights, not civil unions, because the latter would make them second class citizens. She also spoke about the pending New York court case. I advised her that she may want to wait because some of the judges are conservative and likely to vote against marriage equality. She said, "When you are in love with someone, you don't want to wait to start your life together."

She then sent me to a gathering at an Episcopal church in Middletown, New York to meet MENY board members Michael Sabatino and his husband Robert Voorheis. They told me that when they got married out of state, the Catholic Church asked them to leave the choir they belonged to. They left and joined an Episcopal choir. All of this inspired me, and I realized most of MENY's activities were in New York City and we needed outreach into upstate New York. I proposed to Cathy that we hold a rally in the Hudson Valley in Beacon, New York. She made me the outreach coordinator and gave me the green light for the rally.

I worked with Pete Seeger's Beacon Sloop Club and they helped me set up the event in Beacon's Riverside Park. I promoted the event by faxing and emailing press releases for the event to newspapers and radio stations throughout the Hudson Valley over and over again.

On the day of the event, July 6, 2006, Cathy, Michael, Robert, board member

above

Hudson Valley
Assemblyman Frank
Skartados Marriage
Equality Citation.

29

Rob Lassegue and I met at the park and set up our tables and literature in the middle of the park, expecting thousands. Two people showed up. The park was empty, the event was a failure and I worried that the group was upset with me. They were not, but everyone's spirits were down. Then the sloop club took us out on their sailboat and we had a bull session. We decided that instead of creating our own festivals, we would set up tables at established festivals in the region.

Around this time, we had lost the court case and were now working with Governor David Paterson on legalizing marriage equality. On the day of the vote I was at work following Michael's Facebook posts live from the state senate. The assembly had passed the bill and Paterson would sign it into law if the Senate passed it. The vote was close, but the Republicans all decided against and we lost.

I then realized that we needed to work with Republicans on the matter and so I set up a meeting with Cathy and a Hudson Valley Republican leader I knew, John Faso. They talked and it was the first contact with the Republicans by MENY. It started a dialogue.

During this time, I was writing a Room Eight column and hosting a radio segment where I educated people on marriage equality and used those channels to put pressure on my local Hudson Valley Republican Senator Stephen Saland. He was also being lobbied by Big Gay Hudson Valley, a LGBT rights and social organization, his own family, and his rabbi. By now Governor Andrew Cuomo was in office and it was a whole new dynamic thanks to his take-charge attitude towards politics. On the day of the Senate vote I was at home watching the proceedings on TV. Again it was a close vote; and then my Senator, Stephen Saland, got up and gave a passionate speech, voted yes, and we won. I was in tears for the senator's speech, and when he cast the deciding vote, I became a sobbing mess. Echoing Cathy's sentiment some ten years back, we didn't have to wait any longer.

A few years later, Hudson Valley Assemblyman Frank Skartados issued an official citation citing the event in the park and Saland's deciding vote. The document now proudly lives in the research collection of the Poughkeepsie Library. ∞

Kim and Maureen (and Bruce Springsteen):
My Personal Introduction to Marriage Equality

— BILLY BRADFORD

I met my friends Kim and Maureen through Bruce Springsteen. I'm a huge Bruce Springsteen fan. The Internet was very different in those days, and one of the things we used was chat boards. I went to a Bruce Springsteen chat board where there were people organizing tailgate parties for Springsteen concerts in other cities and I said, "Oh, I'll do that!" So, I typed something along the lines of, "I'm going to the Springsteen concert at the Oakland Arena; come to my car and we'll do this!" Maureen was one of the people who came — I met her and her partner Kim and we became fast friends. Many of us who met that day have stayed friends and still go to concerts together. But it was different with Maureen and Kim. I just loved them. I'd go to their house for dinner and we'd go to shows and other events together; they were just a great couple.

In 2004 I was at work in the San Francisco Financial District and Maureen called me at work and asked, "Have you heard the news? [Then San Francisco Mayor] Gavin Newsom is marrying gay couples! Can you get out of work and come to City Hall!?" And, I did! I stopped and got some flowers and met them there. I was the ring bearer and flower girl and witness.

This is so emotional, remembering this … I remember the lines of hundreds of people everywhere — Gavin was walking down the line shaking hands and hugging people. People were laughing and crying. There were florist services coming in and handing out flowers — total strangers from all over the country were calling them and ordering flowers and telling them, "Give to them to people, give them to couples who are marrying." Food was being brought in. After each couple married, they would go outside and crowds were cheering for them. It was just crazy. I mean, it was 2004 — it was

above

Maureen and Kim at
Francisco City Hall.
(2004)

31

like, "How is this happening!?"

At the time we didn't know just how historic this was. Maybe on some level we did, but not really. At the time we didn't know all these people would marry, and then their marriages would get invalidated, and then we'd go to court for the next seven years. At the time it was like, "Gay people can get married – how wonderful!"

(Those approximately 4,000 San Francisco marriages were invalidated by the California Supreme Court in August of 2004. In May 2008 the California Supreme Court ruled that same-sex couples in California could legally marry. Some 18,000+ California same-sex couples rushed to marry. In November 2008 Proposition 8 passed, preventing any further same-sex couples from getting married. In June 2013 the U.S. Supreme Court, in Hollingsworth v. Perry, ruled that the petitioners did not have standing to appeal to the U.S. Court of Appeals for the Ninth Circuit because that court did not have jurisdiction to reach a decision on the case. Therefore, the lower court's ruling stood and gay couples were allowed to legally marry in California.)

Sadly, my friend Maureen died of cancer before she could legally marry Kim again. After her death, Maureen's family made sure that Kim got nothing from their eight-year relationship. Nothing. They treated Kim as though she and Maureen had just been casual friends. That didn't happen to straight couples, only to gay couples. That's when I, personally, fully understood the importance of marriage and why we must work for marriage equality. ∞

n and Maureen
(and Bruce
Springsteen):
My Personal
Introduction to
rriage Equality

BILLY BRADFORD

Billy and Molly Sittin' in a Truck ...

— BILLY BRADFORD

In 2008, when I was putting together Prop 8 rallies in my community, I was watching the local news one day and saw that a rally was taking place at San Francisco City Hall. I immediately ran down to BART to go to the City to help out. I met Stuart Gaffney [then MEUSA Media Team and San Francisco Chapter Leader] as we were coming up out of BART at the Civic Center station. He had a Marriage Equality USA sign in his hand. I asked, "Is this the right direction?" and he said it was.

I went to the rally and I was just a face in the crowd, but I remember wondering: "Who are these people? How do they know where to go and what to do? How is any of this happening? I want to get involved!" (At the time, I was doing small street-corner rallies and sign-holding events at home in Castro Valley, but I wasn't connected with the larger picture.)

At the end of the rally, after the crowd had cleared out, I was standing around talking with Stuart Milk, Harvey Milk's nephew, and a local activist named Kelly Rivera-Hart. I asked them, "How did people know to come here?" Kelly told me to "friend" him on Facebook, which was relatively new at the time. Kelly told me, "Everybody knows to come to things like this through social media, through Facebook." So, I opened a Facebook account. And, I think it was on Facebook that I discovered Marriage Equality USA (MEUSA).

I went on to meet Molly [former MEUSA Media Director and board member Molly McKay] and Davina [former MEUSA Executive Director Davina Kotulski] and the rest is history.

I became known as the person who would do Molly's bidding. Which was fine – she was on stage and I was the one who made sure she had everything she

left–right

The legendary red J⟨ of Equality.

The MEUSA gang fr⟨ out of jail.

33

needed: I arranged permits for events, provided the sound system and other equipment, loaded us in for events, set everything up, engineered the sound, then took everything down and make sure we were all packed to load out.

So, this all began when Molly had ordered some shirts, those blue MEUSA t-shirts we had years ago. She'd ordered them from some place south of Market. She needed help picking them up so she reached out to me, and I said, "Sure!" Molly worked right around the corner from where I did, so after work she picked me up in her Honda Civic. We go to this huge place, and we walk up to the second floor, and there are like 30 GIANT boxes of shirts – like thousands of shirts! And, I'm like, "Wait! What? What are we doing?" And, she's like, "We're picking up these shirts." Very cheerfully and matter-of-factly. I'm, "We're picking up these huge cartons of thousands of shirts in what, your Honda Civic? Did you think this through?"

So, we loaded up maybe five boxes of shirts, whatever we could cram into her little Honda Civic, and the next day I had to go rent a U-Haul truck and go back to get all the rest of the shirts. And, I had to go by myself because Molly couldn't get off work. And, I thought I was taking the shirts to the Marriage Equality USA office, but it turned out there wasn't an office, which I didn't know. And, Molly couldn't fit all these shirts into her little house on a hill in Oakland, so the shirts needed to be stored in my garage. For months I couldn't park my car in the garage because the garage was filled with Marriage Equality USA t-shirts!

The shirts were eventually distributed to all these other people, chapter leaders. Then, a couple of years later, I went back out to collect the shirts that hadn't been used. Molly called, "Billy, I need you to do this." And, I'm like, "Okay!" and off I went, alone, with a truck, to like 10 different houses all around the Bay Area in one day, to pick up the remaining shirts.

So, that became the thing. Billy's house, Billy's Legendary Garage of Equality, Billy's Red Jeep of Equality, and wherever Molly was Billy was there with a truck.

And, that was Molly! She was always like, "We got this. Of course, we can do this!" Very positive. Very full of energy. Picking up the shirts was one of those moments when, here's this person you hold in high esteem, and all of a sudden you have to step back and look at them in a different way. You still love them, but you learn to ask more questions! Davina and I used to trail along behind Molly asking questions, "Did she get her purse? Do we have a permit for this? Do we have the bullhorn? Where are we going? What are we doing? Do we need sound? Do we need a truck? Does anyone know how to get there?" Molly just forged ahead and someone else needed to ask the questions and cover the details. Molly is awesome, I love her! ∞

*Billy and Moll_*
Sittin' in a Tru

BILLY BRADFORD

35

Every Moment of an Action Is Important

– KATE BURNS

November 2006 was a time of heartbreaking news for many lesbian and gay Coloradans. The religious right and ultra-conservative politicians passed a "marriage = man + woman" amendment to the state constitution. And the humble counter-initiative, Referendum I, developed by LGBTQ leaders to preserve a few rights for non-heterosexual couples, was soundly defeated. The trauma of that double blow seemed to knock the wind out of activism. Out of the agonizing stillness, a dozen or so of us formed a local group led by Chris Hubble that was associated with the international Soulforce movement, dedicated to ending religious and political oppression of LGBTQ people through relentless nonviolent resistance. Our group created vigils, direct-actions, and acts of civil disobedience in the shadow of the fundamentalist mega-organization Focus on the Family, headquartered in Colorado Springs.

Focus on the Family had sponsored the campaign to prevent any form of legal recognition for Colorado lesbian and gay couples. We decided to develop a protest that exposed the symbiotic connection between Focus on the Family and Colorado politicians. On September 24, 2007, my spouse, Sheila Schroeder, and I walked into the Denver County Marriage License office, hand-in-hand with our Unitarian Universalist Minister, Rev. Mike Morran. Since so much of the anti-queer effort had been driven by the religious right we knew it was important to have a clergy member with us to show that religion in America is not owned by conservative fundamentalism.

The first half hour of the action was electrifying. We had alerted the media, and were surprised by the amount of media attention we actually got: six television cameras, three newspaper photographers, and reporters from little

36

neighborhood newspapers all the way to the New York Times. The cameras popped their flashes each time we did something significant: when we asked for a marriage license, showed our drivers licenses, kissed each other with the anticipation of being newlyweds, explained our pain and anger when we could not receive the same benefits that thousands of other taxpayers receive in the same office, and then, when we sat down in protest in front of the counter after being refused a license.

Every Moment of an Action Is Important

KATE BURNS

Since we were blocking only one of the three counters, the County Clerk tolerated our sit-in. The camera operators put their heavy loads down and sat in a semi-circle around us. Sheila began to talk to the reporters and photographers, asking them about their families and relationships. We all sat together for an hour, sharing stories and joking. At one point a cameraman paused and said, "My fiancée and I will be getting married next month. I don't see any reason why you two shouldn't be able to get married, too. I wish that you could have the same sense of anticipation that I have today – the comforting thought that I'll be putting a ring on the finger of the one I love soon." Many of the other reporters and photographers murmured their agreement. Tears sprang to our eyes at the reminder that every moment of an action is important – not just the dramatic, camera-flashing moments.

The dramatic moment did come when the office closed and we refused to leave without receiving what was rightfully ours – our marriage license. The Clerk called the police, and we were read our rights, handcuffed, and hauled into police cruisers. Rounding the corner in the back of the squad car, we saw about a hundred supporters holding signs and waving to honking cars passing by, bringing a new wave of tears to our eyes.

We were booked for trespassing and then released, and thought the action was over. But we soon found that we could keep the issue alive by making a media-worthy action of each of our numerous court appearances. The law firm of Killmer, Lane & Newman took our case pro bono, with Mari Newman as lead counsel.

After our lawyers argued fiercely for cameras to be allowed in the courtroom, the trial began. Our lawyers mounted a strong defense for us, arguing that we were forced to commit a lesser crime – trespassing – in order to enforce a higher law, the Constitution. We knew that this "lesser evil" defense was a long shot, but it allowed us to talk about why we were in the marriage license office in the first place, something that wouldn't have been allowed if our defense merely addressed the trespassing charge. The television stations aired our story that evening.

At trial's end, we were found guilty. We asked to address the court before sentencing. "Your Honor," I said, "if you are considering jail time or fines, we ask you to commute as much as you can to community service hours. We did this out of a love for our community and the belief that our actions would ultimately benefit the county, our state, and our nation. Please let us continue to serve our community – we would welcome such a sentence!" He complied and gave us each 28 hours of community service.

We found out that our Colorado LGBT Center was among the hundreds of organizations where we could perform community service hours. Hooray! We served our sentence by organizing a fundraiser for the Center. We put on a screening of our film, SoleJourney, a documentary about the Soulforce movement. Over 300 people attended, raising $1,500 for the Center. And of course we made sure the media was there to keep the issue in the public eye once again.

We planned another civil disobedience action in 2009, that time with five participants. We spent an evening in jail and some of us received harsher sentences. I served my new sentence of 40 hours of community service by recording oral history videos for our local PFLAG organization. Again, I saw that serving time could help the cause.

Thanks to the marriage equality movement, I have learned to take a broad view when it comes to activism – to anticipate and utilize the hundred small opportunities to make change along with the big events. Activism encompasses not just the dramatic demonstrations or direct actions, but the whole journey. ∞

This Is What DOMA Does to People – It Shatters Their Lives

– MARVIN BURROWS

Marvin Burrows was a long time member of Marriage Equality USA, serving as the Community Liaison for Seniors. Marvin showed up at every rally, even at times when he should have stayed home and taken care of himself. He carried signs, did interviews, spoke at the state capitol, lobbied politicians, and traveled around the state, so that never again would an LGBT widow or widower face homelessness, lose their health insurance, or be told by a funeral home director that they are "not family." Marvin died on December 14, 2013 after finally seeing the Defense of Marriage Act and Prop 8 struck down by the U.S. Supreme Court in June 2013. On July 20, 2011 he testified for the U.S. Senate Judiciary Committee on the harmful effects of DOMA. These are his words...

I respectfully address the United States Senate Judiciary Committee:

My name is Marvin Burrows, and I am 75 years old. I live in Hayward, California. I was born and spent my childhood in Michigan. I served in the United States Air Force.

My parents knew I was homosexual by the time I was 15 years old. They decided to put me in a "mental home" to be "cured" of this dreaded "disease." I tried to hang myself so my family wouldn't have to be embarrassed that I was a queer. After the suicide attempt, instead of being committed, I was given the choice to do outpatient therapy. The physiatrist told my mom and me that my treatment would be different than we expected. He helped me learn how to live in society and how to protect myself. Considering the times, the early 1950s, that doctor was a true exception! I believe that without his help I would not be alive today.

left–right

Marvin and Bill are married at San Fran City Hall in February 2004.

Stuart Gaffney, Mar Burrows, and Kirste Berzon at Oakland September 1, 2013.
Photo credit: Levi Smith Photography

39

This Is What
DOMA Does
to People —
It Shatters
Their Lives

MARVIN BURROWS

I met the love of my life, William Duane Swenor, in 1953. He was 15 and I was 17. My father found out and told me to leave home if I continued to see Bill. After my dad kicked me out I had no place to go, and I was still in high school. I stayed with my grandmother until Bill could ask his mother if I could move in with them. She gave her permission, I moved in, and from that time on we lived as a committed couple.

I had limited contact with my family, with the exception of my mother and grandmother. Finally, after a very long time, the rest of my family accepted Bill as my life partner.

Bill and I moved from Michigan to California in the mid '60s because we thought we would be more accepted in San Francisco.

We bought things jointly, we opened joint bank accounts. We shared all of our income and expenses. We rented apartments together, but often had to lie about our relationship, even to the point of telling potential landlords that we were related.

We did the best we could at the time to protect our relationship, drawing up legal papers in case of illness, injury or death. We had wills, powers of attorney, and advance directives. We spent a good deal of money and time trying to protect what we had built together.

When the California State Domestic Partners Registry became available in 2000, Bill and I registered. We were told that our registration would take the place of the Powers of Attorney, and to our knowledge our relationship was then legally protected.

On February 15, 2004 Bill and I married when Mayor Gavin Newsom of San Francisco gave us the opportunity. At that time we had been together for 50 years. We were very surprised at how emotional we became while saying our vows. To be able to speak those words, out loud, in front of others, brought tears to our eyes. It was the best time in our lives and we had high hopes for our future as a married couple. I have attached a photograph of our wedding to this statement. I am on the left in the photo, and Bill is on the right.

Without a doubt, that ceremony changed and revitalized our relationship. It gave us an important measure of pride and acceptance. It felt great to be able to do something so personal, and yet so historic, all at the same time.

However, our marriage and over 4,000 others were declared null and void by the California Supreme Court six months later, in August of 2004.

When the California Supreme Court declared, in May of 2008, that we California same-sex couples could get legally married at long last, it was too late for Bill and me.

Had we had the chance to marry legally under California law, we would have done so. But Bill died of a heart attack on March 7, 2005. I was completely devastated.

While Bill was alive he had signed me up for his union insurance through the International Longshore and Warehouse Union (ILWU). Bill had to pay income taxes on that insurance, even though straight married couples do not have pay such taxes. Bill had also signed me up for his pension benefits through the ILWU. When he died, however, I was told that due to DOMA I was denied Bill's pension. I was told this twice to my face and several other times in letters sent to people who were trying to help me. Three years later, after years of fighting with the help of the National Center for Lesbian Rights, the union finally changed its position and gave me Bill's pension, saying it was "the right thing to do for a fellow member."

I also could not collect Social Security benefits based on Bill's earnings, even though, had Bill married five different women in the 51 years we were together, each one of them could have claimed his Social Security. We both paid into the Social Security system. We shared everything and loved only each other for our entire adult lives. It is unfair, and it is un-American that I should be left this way by our country.

I had to move from our home of 35 years because I could no longer afford the payments without his Social Security benefits. I could not live on my own as I was almost financially destitute, so a friend invited me to move into his home. I lost my cat and had to give away our pet parrots. I didn't even have room to keep our bedroom set, so I gave that to my nephew. I lost my lifelong partner, my home, our animals, income, my health insurance, and even my bed and furniture all in one fell swoop.

This Is What
DOMA Does
to People –
It Shatters
Their Lives

MARVIN BURROWS

All of this would have happened to me, even if Bill had lived long enough for us to marry.

The reason is the Defense of Marriage Act. Bill still would have been taxed on health benefits for me, I still would not have received Bill's Social Security, I would have had to fight for years for Bill's pension, and I would have lost my house.

This is what DOMA does to people. It shatters their lives at a time when they need stability and comfort the most. It makes people, including me, feel like less of a person – like an outcast not worthy of full equality.

I still believe that this country can change for the better, and I do my best to contribute to my community on a volunteer basis. For example, I have volunteered to deliver Meals on Wheels for 22 years, and I am a founder of Lavender Seniors of the East Bay. I do believe that we will be allowed to marry some day in every state, and I believe these marriages will be recognized by our federal government.

It may not happen in my lifetime, but it gives me great hope to believe that someday no one will have to go through what I did when I lost the love of my life. I hope my story will open the minds of the Committee members and other members of Congress to repealing DOMA and treating gay couples equally. ∞

Yes, I'm About to Ruin My Political Career

— GEOFF CALLAN & MIKE SHAW

I didn't expect that making the documentary film *Pursuit of Equality* would change my life. In fact, I and my co-director Mike Shaw hadn't planned to make a film at all. We had no script, shooting schedule, cast of characters, or even a budget. Frankly, we really didn't understand the issue at hand. Like most people, we had no idea what was about to transpire during San Francisco's "Winter of Love." We were just two tenacious filmmakers at the right place at the right time.

It all began innocently enough over brunch on February 8, 2004, with a few members of my family and my brother-in-law Gavin Newsom, the newly-elected mayor of San Francisco. I asked, almost jokingly, if there was anything exciting going on, and he said, "Yes, I'm about to ruin my political career." I pressed him, but he wouldn't explain further. He just said that what he was about to do "was the right thing to do." On the evening of February 11, 2004, Gavin called me at home and asked that Mike and I film the first official same-sex wedding in California, when Del Martin and Phyllis Lyon would be married. Game on!

The next day, Mike and I arrived at City Hall at 7:30 a.m. The press was completely unaware, and there were only a few key members of the mayor's staff on hand, alongside a few high-powered members of the LGBT community. We had no idea that, as Del and Phyllis exchanged their vows, this moment would ignite what would become the most controversial United States civil rights topic in recent history.

The City continued to marry gay and lesbian couples, and we faithfully kept the cameras rolling. Over the next month, with a meager crew and no budget, we religiously charged our batteries, cleaned our lenses, and remained singularly focused on filming these historic events. We filmed in the streets, in

top–bottom

Director Mike Shaw
Francisco Mayor Ga
Newsom, Director G
Callan. (2005)
Photo credit: Drew Alti

Pursuit of Equality f
poster.

43

the courtrooms, and found ourselves the only film crew in the actual Mayor's Chambers. On the steps of City Hall, we witnessed clashes between same-sex couples on the happiest day of their lives, with church groups declaring those couples enmeshed in a life of sin and shame. We documented the elation (and later, despair) of couples and families fighting for their right to protect each other.

We sacrificed all of our other clients' film and television projects to keep filming. We sensed that we had the power to make a difference and to expand people's hearts and minds. We had to make this film.

The California Supreme Court issued an immediate halt to marriage licenses on March 11, 2004, after over 3,900 couples had already been married in the state. The marriages were annulled, confiscating the joy and validation of thousands of couples. The news cameras clicked off and their sound bites ceased. It was then that our real journey began, as our cameras continued to roll. We continued to document this issue for the next 19 months. Just when we'd finish one version of the film, a new legal development or court decision would outdate it. We locked in a final film cut in late 2007, setting for a 2008 release date.

On May 15, 2008, the California State Supreme Court ruled in a historic 4–3 decision that gays and lesbians have a constitutional right to marry in California. California Chief Justice Ronald George declared in the majority opinion that "an individual's sexual orientation – like a person's race or gender – does not constitute a legitimate basis upon which to deny or withhold legal rights."

Much has happened since 2008, and today, same-sex marriage is the law of the land. Nevertheless, our society remains fractured over this issue, with many Americans against same-sex marriage or on the fence. The intent of our film *Pursuit of Equality* is to present with honesty the many sides of the same-sex marriage debate, while at the same time putting a human face on discrimination. Educating people on this issue is vital, and now, more than ever, is the time to share *Pursuit of Equality* with all of our friends, family, and colleagues. The fight continues. ∞

Blazing an Equality Caravan Across America

— FRANK & JOE CAPLEY-ALFANO

When same-sex couples gained the right to marry in Massachusetts, Frank and I made plans to be there when it happened. It was 2004, and we had been a part of the Winter-of-Love in San Francisco. In fact, we were even lucky enough to have the opportunity to be married at SF City Hall, but the legality of the marriage certificates was questionable at best. The first truly legal same-sex marriages in the United States were going to happen in Massachusetts later that year, and we wanted to be present to bear witness and be a part of history in the making. What is more, Frank had never been to Boston, so we took a few extra days there, and we did a little sightseeing.

For the first time in our lives, we were truly filled with national pride and joy. We, same-sex couples, were going to be included in the American Dream (at least in Massachusetts) and it felt great! So, we hit the Freedom Trail, to revel in our nation's progressive history and the American Revolution for Independence. If you don't know, the Freedom Trail is literally a line painted on the ground that you follow around downtown Boston from one historic tourist site to the next. We went to the Old North Church, Faneuil Hall, the Old State House, and the Paul Revere House. Revere was a Freemason like me, and I felt really akin to him and the other Masons that led the way in the revolution and the founding of these United States.

On the Trail, we passed several other historic sites that have Masonic significance. One location, the Green Dragon Tavern, is a 200-year-old tavern that used to house a Masonic Lodge upstairs, where the Boston Tea Party was actually planned. We stopped in to rest our feet, to have a nostalgic beer, and to toast my long dead brethren for their belief in fraternity, liberty and equal-

above

Frank and Joe in fr
the Marriage Equa
Express Bus. (200

left–right

Frank and Joe in W
ington D.C. at the d
of the Marriage Eq
Express. (2004)

Frank and Joe on t
"Freedom Trail" in B
during their trip to
legally married in
sachusetts. (2004

Frank and Joe in W
ington D.C. at the
of the Marriage Eq
Express for the firs
tional rally for mar
equality. (2004)

45

ity that led them to put their lives on the line to fight tyranny and oppression. Honestly, the tavern was kind of dark, so we sat up front, where there were seats adjacent to open sets of windows which faced out onto the street and Freedom Trail. We were enjoying our beers, the rest, and nostalgia, when a chance encounter led to a cross country bus trip, a crash course in public speaking and marriage law, many close friendships, and an 11-year struggle for marriage equality that became a revolution in itself.

Molly McKay and Davina Kotulski, leaders in the movement to secure legal marriage for same-sex couples in California, turned the corner. We'd met during the Winter of Love in San Francisco, and we recognized one another immediately. I think that they were as shocked or more to see us, as we were to see them, and we ran outside to give them big hugs. We asked if they had also been in Cambridge, which was the first locale to give out marriage licenses at 12:01 a.m. on May 17th. It was absolutely amazing, and I will never forget the feeling of camaraderie and joy that I felt with those around me in attendance that night. Molly and Davina said yes, they had been in Cambridge; but there were so many people at the Cambridge City Hall that the police had to close the streets for several blocks in each direction, so it wasn't surprising that we didn't see them. In fact, in all of the jubilation, I lost my "Newly-Weds, Married in San Francisco" button, that was given to us by Shelly Bailes and Ellen Pontac, who soon thereafter would become bus-mates, long term fellow activists, and good friends. Coincidentally, as I was searching the ground for my lost pin, I found another one that was shaped like a heart that had presumably been lost by someone from Massachusetts. It had "We Made History! Celebrate Gay Marriage" printed on it, and finding it made me feel better about losing mine. I hope that the person who found mine felt good too.

Molly and Davina asked if we wanted to join them and 45 others on a cross country bus trip, to speak about why marriage was important to us. The trip would come to be known as the Marriage Equality Express Caravan,¹ and it followed in the footsteps of the 1960's Freedom Riders. We were elated, and we said yes immediately. I don't even think that we hesitated for a moment, but then, I am not sure that we really even gave deep consideration to what they were actually proposing, what it would take to make it happen, or the potential threat of physical harm that could come to us in response to our actions. Earnestly, none of that mattered. This was an opportunity of a lifetime and the kind of thing that stories are written about years later!

At the time, the Marriage Express Caravan was cutting edge queer politics, an army of Love Warriors on a national campaign that culminated in a national rally at the U.S. Capitol. Little did we know what we were really getting ourselves into. In six days, we crossed the country, covered nine states and the District of Columbia. The bus was our classroom, and the team of organizers taught a curriculum that included marriage facts and law, essays to be written, and speeches to give. Through the process, we found our story, the essence of why marriage mattered to us, and we honed our speaking skills by practicing our stories for hours among our captive audience. With every mile and every stop, we became a little more comfortable with our knowledge of the materials and our ability to speak concisely in public. In short, our ragtag group of naive idealists quickly became a strong core group of educated, outspoken, and engaged marriage equality activists. Consequently, we came to know our fellow riders and their narratives intimately too. In truth, by the end of the trip, we became a well oiled machine and kindred spirits; in many ways, we became a family.

In each state, we stopped in one or two cities, meeting with supporting communities in each locale, and often, we passed through more than one state a day. At some spots, we held large rallies, and sometimes, where communities still couldn't be open for threat of physical harm, losing their jobs, or homes, we gathered in smaller groups, with affirming congregations or at a community nonprofit. Once, it was just us. We had a scheduled stop at the University of Wyoming, which is just outside of Laramie, where Matthew Shepard was murdered. Many of us wanted to make pilgrimage to the spot where Matthew died, and to the Fireside Lounge, where his killers picked him up. The affirming clergy among us suggested having a prayer for Matthew and for peace, and we descended into the valley, where Laramie and the Fireside sit. There wasn't a cloud in the sky when we exited the freeway and made our way toward the Fireside, but by the time we reached our destination the sky had covered over with clouds and the wind had picked up. I remember standing as a group near the front door of the vacant building under the roof of the exterior patio. Because of the wind, we had a really hard time lighting candles that were to be a part of our ceremony, and when we began our collective prayer, the sky opened up and released torrents of rain and then hail. It was like Matthew was sending a message to us, or he was welling up with emotion and crying along with the rest of us. Many riders spoke of their own experiences of being shamed and bashed for being LGBTQIA. It was lugubrious and somber, and as the last speaker uttered her final words, the precipitation ceased. As we boarded the bus, the clouds began to clear, and as we climbed slowly out of valley for UW the sky was clear again, and we had all been profoundly affected by the unusual experience.

Each stop-over was equally unique, and each encounter along the way was truly moving for all involved. We spoke our truths, and we listened to the stories of our hosts. We heard testimony of life experience, much like our own, that all too often ended in tragedy because same-sex couples weren't allowed access to legal marriage. With each attestation, our motivation and conviction to secure marriage for all solidified, and by the time our bus reached Washington, D.C., we had really become a force to be reckoned with, and we weren't going to be stopped.

We learned that our stories had real power, and that by speaking out about the truths of our experience, we could connect with others in a very human way. By doing so, they often related to our commonality, if even in just a small way. Telling our stories became our battle cries, and we told them time and again for the next 11 years to all who would listen and to some that just wouldn't. Heck, we even told each other's stories, and most of the time, love conquered hate. That's not to say that there weren't a whole lotta bumps along the way, because I can recall some very low and scary points. But the bonds that we formed, the principles that we established, and the determination that we shared kept our hearts steadfast, as we transformed obstacles into cobblestones and paved a rainbow path to marriage equality thereby extend-

48

ing our nation's collective freedom trail a little bit further. In the end, love prevailed. ∞

—

1 The "Marriage Equality Express" (2004) was a cross-country bus caravan organized and attended by MEUSA and other marriage equality activists in response to the invalidation of over 4,000 marriages performed during the San Francisco 2004 "Winter of Love." Designed to provide education and awareness in communities across the country, the bus tour culminated at the first national rally for marriage equality in Washington D.C. on 11 October 2004.

FRANK & JOE
CAPLEY-ALFANO

The Day I Found MEUSA
and the Day That Changed My Life

— SEAN CHAPIN

November 5, 2008. I woke up that morning, and I pretty much knew. I didn't have to go online or turn on the T.V. Many people had started the day with the greatest hope they felt in their lives. But I and others woke up with our hopes threatened.

The night before, my friend and I were watching CNN at his place in the Castro. In a pivotal moment, the network acknowledged the polls closing in California and other Western states at the 8 o'clock hour, and right afterward called for Barack Obama to be our next President. We immediately screamed for joy. My friend's apartment door was open, and the sound of elation from the neighborhood poured into his space. We ran out onto his balcony that overlooked the Market and Castro intersection, and we felt the amazing buzz. We hollered out toward the Castro Theater, adding our own excitement to the mix. Within an hour, this vibrant energy transformed into a Castro Street party with people flooding the streets and dancing to music, celebrating a new President, and ushering in a hopeful era of politics.

At the same time, returns started coming in for another major election issue – California's Proposition 8, which would ban the right of same-sex marriage directly in the state's constitution. As they continued coming in over the next hour, the outlook of this ballot initiative looked progressively bleaker for the side of equality, and whatever happiness I felt for the Presidential outcome was quickly washing away. Discouraged, I walked by the block party on my way home. Looking at the party-goers while passing by, I wanted to ask them all: "How can you dance for joy when something really scary is about to happen to us?"

The next morning was a stark contrast to the night before. The Castro was quiet, almost solemn, with very few people around. The sky was scattered with gloomy gray clouds. And the great Castro rainbow flag, a beacon of Harvey Milk's hope given by its creator, Gilbert Baker, many years before, was restrained at half-mast, while in its place above was a black stripe of a flag, clumsily and dishearteningly flying in the wind. I had just left my place a minute before when I heard about the flag on the radio, so I decided to turn around back home and grab my video camera and tripod to bring with me.

I drove over to the Castro, and I heard the quiet solemnity, and saw the heartbreaking display of the flag and black stripe. I set up my tripod and pressed record on my video camera, and I stood there while the camera and I took it in. The rainbow flag would try to dance with the wind, but couldn't. It was the black stripe's job to do so for the day. The neighborhood was stricken and weeping. Our vulnerability was there for everyone in the area to see.

A half hour later I arrived at work, and I made a phone call to my boyfriend before stepping inside. I wasn't the only one in my immediate life feeling this grief – he lived in Florida, which on the same day passed Amendment 2 and outlawed same-sex marriage in that state's Constitution. And these two states were only half the story. A third state, Arizona, had done something similar, while a fourth state, Arkansas, outlawed gay couples and other unmarried couples from adopting children. It was one thing for California to feel such an incredible sting; however, with four states at once being affected legally from the election, the entire nation was feeling an intensified threat of homophobia. My boyfriend in Florida answered my call, and he sounded devastated. Ordinarily, we would feel very happy to talk to each other and hear each other's voices. That morning, we instead felt intense sadness and hopelessness, and we commiserated for a few minutes before we got on with our days on our sides of the country, or at least tried to.

It was hard to focus at work that day. Just months before, in May, California had legalized marriage equality, and it was an epiphany for me. For over a decade, since I came out at 17, I had resigned myself to living a sub-par life as a gay man with partial rights and opportunities. On that day in May, I started feeling a much bigger dream of living with full equality and freedom in this country; and yet here I was six months later, in front of my work computer screen, overcome with sadness, fear, and anger. Sadness, because I was losing this newfound marriage right after getting only a proverbial second to taste it. Fear, because countless people were able to exercise a power to render me less equal to them solely because of who I am. And for the first time, anger, because I knew more than ever before that I deserved the very equality that was being taken away from me.

I decided to hop onto Facebook at some point, and I saw a friend's post about a rally that was taking place that evening. People were going to gather outside of the San Francisco City Hall building for a candlelight vigil and rally. I noticed a few people I know sign up for this event, which was being organized by a group called Marriage Equality USA. I was normally averse to participating in these kind of gatherings, but on an extraordinary day like this, I felt a need to be among others who were going through similar feelings as I was, and I didn't want to be alone.

It was 6:00 p.m. when I arrived and made my way toward the front steps of City Hall, carrying my video camera and a new candle. There were about 25 people standing together on the steps facing the street, many of them holding up signs about marriage equality and renouncing Prop 8. Others were gathering on the sidewalk facing this group of sign-holders, and I decided to stand with them. As people continued to gather, we all stood there quiet for the most part, unless a car driving by honked at us, which got many people to cheer back … this happened a little more and more, as if a snowball was just beginning its unbeknownst descent down a gradual, historic mountainside.

Within a half hour, the sun's twilight rays left the city, and the crowd's size was steadily multiplying. People all around me were starting to light their candles. I had both hands busy, with one carrying my candle, and another holding my video camera; thankfully, someone was nice enough to light my candle for me.

I had started filming a few minutes after I arrived. I filmed the sign-holders in front of me, the people all around me, the United States flag waving above the steps, the beautiful architecture of the San Francisco City Hall, the lit candles everywhere. Still holding up my lit candle, I kept on filming, eventually getting lost behind the camera's view screen as the evening progressed. When the rally started, over a thousand people had gathered, covering the entire width of the City Hall steps, spreading far across the sidewalk and even spilling over to the other side of Polk Street.

I heard a number of speakers that evening, and I heard others lead the crowd in a few songs. I hadn't heard of many of the speakers or singers before. One speaker proclaimed, "No more talk about them and us – we are us!" Another, a politician representing the Castro district, resolved to fight back until this discrimination was taken back out of California's state constitution. A pastor from a local church had the crowd clapping and singing, "Ain't gonna let nobody turn me around. Turn me around, turn me around. Ain't gonna let nobody turn me around. Keep on walking. Keep on talking. Marching up to freedom land … Ain't gonna let Prop 8 turn me around. Turn me around, turn me around. Ain't gonna let Prop 8 turn me around. Keep on walking. Keep on talking. Marching up to freedom land."

Another singer, a leader from Marriage Equality USA, performed a beautiful version of "I Know Where I've Been" from the movie Hairspray. "There's a light in the darkness, though the night is black and it's dim. There's a light burning bright, showing me the way." "Sing, girl!" someone next to me shouted, while others around her clapped enthusiastically as the singer continued behind the microphone.

Throughout that evening, amidst the sadness, fear and anger that I had been processing earlier, I discovered a new, stronger feeling: courage. I had woken up that morning with my hope threatened, but here I was hours later, our hope lighting the way as we stood together outside our City Hall. I was realizing a resilience that I never knew had existed within me, and I was starting to feel more empowered than I could fathom. Little did I know at the time how far that empowerment would take me.

On that evening in front of the City Hall steps, it was the Marriage Equality USA organization and so many rally gatherers who connected to me in a powerful way and awakened my voice to join theirs. Within the rally, I could feel all of us find each other, our energy binding us, helping us start to heal and overcome the horrible strife that Prop 8 wrought upon us and giving us strength and courage to come out like we hadn't before and fight back for equality. People raised their lit candles to the powerful words of the speakers and singers. Huge signs proclaiming equality and love were scattered throughout and danced up and down with the energy of the crowd.

The singer continued her song ... "Use that pride in our hearts, to lift us up to tomorrow, 'cause just to sit still would be a sin, Lord knows I know, where I've been." The crowd cheered, and cheered ... the cheering never really stopped. It morphed into a loud rallying cry, one heard often during Barack Obama's presidential campaign that year. "Yes we can. Yes we can! Yes we can! Yes we can! Yes we can! Yes we can! Yes we can! Yes we can! Yes we can! Yes we can! Yes we can! Yes we can! Yes we can! Yes we can. Yes we can ..."

I was unaware of what Marriage Equality USA was prior to that evening, but I would get to know this organization and its leaders soon after, volunteering for them as their right-hand videographer at many of their rallies and protests for years to come. At the same time, I would quickly find my own voice in the greater LGBT civil rights movement, one that was both behind the camera as well as in front of it. My voice would carry through my YouTube channel as far as prominent national blogs, the local news channels and sometimes on CNN. A few years later it would even catalyze the local San Francisco Giants baseball team to publicly reach out to LGBT youth and give them hope through the It Gets Better Project.

Over seven years have passed since that day. I'm sitting here at a coffee shop in the Castro, a year after we won our nationwide marriage equality. A few days ago, I was at the 20th anniversary celebration of Marriage Equality USA, as we all came together to reminisce over our transcendent journey together and rejoice in accomplishing our mission of marriage equality across the country. It dumbfounds me how far we have come during these years, and I feel blessed to get to continue forward and fully realize my dream of living with equality. Yes we can, and now, yes I will. ∞

Revolution

— J. SCOTT COATSWORTH

We wanted to be a part of the revolution. But that cold night in Sacramento in November 2008 when we elected the nation's first African American President, we also lost the battle against Prop 8. It felt like the revolution was over.

The long road to getting married started on a warm spring day in March of 2004 in San Francisco – our first wedding. That spring, Gavin Newsom opened the doors of the city clerk's office to the gay and lesbian community, and an air of celebration reigned in the city by the bay.

But one question floated above it all – something that our gay friends recognized instantly when we talk about it, and something that's as foreign to our straight friends as the wilds of Africa.

"Will it count?"

For Mark and me, it was "the" question. For almost a month we went back and forth over whether or not to get married. Yes, we loved each other. Yes, we had always planned to get married eventually, when it was legal. But was it real? Would it be snatched away? Do we throw our hearts into it, and invite our family and friends, only to see it all taken away?

Of all the problems facing our parents when they got married – where to have the ceremony, civil or religious, what flavor to make the cake, and how to seat the guests – "will it count" was never a concern.

In the end, we decided to take the chance. On March 10, we checked the San Francisco clerk's website, and although they had been booked for weeks, there was suddenly an opening the very next day. It felt like it was "meant to be."

So we packed our suitcases, hopped in the car, and drove to the City. We called our parents (talk about uncharted ground), and explained why this

above

Our Wedding Day, S
Francisco. (2008)
Photo credit: Nick Lost

55

was so important to us. We promised to do this again "for real" at a later date, and asked them to come if and when the state finally made it legal. And they all said yes.

We arrived late at City Hall because traffic was so bad, but they took us in anyway.

Looking back, I remember how normal it all felt, and what a wonderful word normal could be. Two perfect strangers were there for us, one to act as our witness, and one as our officiant, free of charge because they'd heard about the weddings and wanted to come do something and to be a part of it all. We said our vows at the top of the grand staircase, under the vaulted dome of city hall, and when we said "I Do," both of us felt a sudden, unexpected rush of connectedness and love as the city of San Francisco recognized our relationship and our marriage.

There's power in recognition.

What had started as a political act for us was suddenly so much more. It meant something. And at that moment, I understood the difference between a "domestic partnership" and a true marriage.

Later that day, the state Supreme Court called a halt to the weddings at last after 26 days – just an hour or two after we were married. And months later, our license was invalidated by that same court. It turned out it didn't "count" after all.

And yet it did, to us.

Four years later, in the spring of 2008, the presidential election was gathering steam. We had just launched Marriage Equality Watch in January.[1] Mark and I were big Hillary fans, but as the race wore on, we started to get excited about the underdog in the race, a young guy from Illinois named Barack Obama. And as he gained momentum, we saw the possibility he represented for both the LGBTIQA community and for the country as a whole.

So we jumped on the Obama bandwagon and donated to the campaign, cast our primary vote, and made campaign calls for our new hope.

Then on June 16, 2008, the California Supreme Court released its ruling, I sat at my desk, logged into the Supreme Court website, hitting refresh over and

56

over and over on my browser at 9:59, 10:00 a.m. ... and suddenly, there it was.

I rushed through the ruling, and when I got to the end I started to cry.

The impossible had happened. The same Court that had torn asunder our marriage license four years before now said we had every right to get married.

I turned to Mark and told him we'd won – we could really get married. It was a moment of utter elation, sheer joy, and unmitigated relief ... but all of these fail to capture the upwelling of emotions we felt. Validation. Vindication. Hope.

But dark clouds were gathering.

People forget that Prop 8 didn't come out of thin air. It was not a reaction to the California Supreme Court decision. At least, not directly. Signature gathering to put it on the ballot had begun the year before, as part of the national effort to codify discrimination into the constitutions of every state. The ruling poured fuel on that hateful fire.

As Mark and I campaigned for Obama, we laughed at the marriage equality opponents. Surely something like that could never pass in California, not in 2008. But our laughter turned to concern and then to outright consternation over that long, hot summer and fall, as the initiative climbed in the polls.

June became July became August became September, and then, all at once, the ads started. Mayor Newsom, sneering "whether you like it or not," trampled all over the ineffective anti-Prop 8 ads showing a bride being tripped at her wedding or a couple of parents talking about their daughter and her partner. As a community, we were asleep at the switch, unable to see what was bearing down upon us. When it hit, it was too late to fight back.

Prop 8's poll numbers started out around 42%. We watched in growing dismay as they climbed to 44%, and then 45%, and then 47%.

We lived in El Dorado Hills at the time, a fairly conservative community, and in October we put up four anti-Prop 8 signs around town. In less than a week, all were taken down by our opponents.

And the lawns and fences in town were awash in a sea of yellow, with thousands of pro-Prop 8 signs drowning our neighborhoods. As autumn progressed, it became painfully clear what a great motivator fear could be.

As Prop 8 rose in the polls, all those familiar questions from four years before came flooding back. Get married now, and risk it being taken away? Or do we wait, and risk losing the chance?

Sometimes, I'd lay awake at night, unable to sleep, and would get up at three in the morning to write an editorial against Prop 8 on the Marriage Equality Watch blog, just to get the anger and fear and sadness out of my head and onto the screen. To be doing something, anything to shout out the truth and try to cut through the thicket of lies and deceptions woven around the issue.

We settled into a sort of wedding-paralysis, and watched the polls, hoping California would get this right.

Mark and I realized in mid-October that our window was quickly closing. Our dream of a big beautiful wedding with all of our family around us was about to be snatched away. If we were to have any chance at getting married legally in California, it had to be then.

In the end, with just three weeks to go before the election, we decided to let go of all of our "big wedding" dreams. If we were going to be married, it had to be now. I remember the day very clearly — sitting with Mark at lunch at our favorite Italian restaurant in Sacramento, talking about what to do next. Once again agonizing over not having the wedding we wanted, this time over gnocchi, chicken saltimbocca and French fries. And looking up at Mark and saying, "What if we invited our parents? What if we made this wedding 'real'? What if we didn't do this alone?" That night, we called them — my mom and dad, and Mark's mom.

I still remember my mom saying, "Of course I'll be there." She had supported me from the day I came out, but there was always that ... pause, when we talked about LGBT issues. And now, at last, the pause was gone. I'd never felt better in my life than I did at that moment.

Some of our relatives were not so supportive. People who had treated us with what seemed like total, loving acceptance. But Prop 8 exposed a divide we had never really been aware of, that we'd all agreed to paper over. They told us they didn't believe in gay marriage, that they only "tolerated" that side of us, and that they would be voting for Prop 8 to take away our marriage rights. It was like an open wound — this sudden, devastating knowledge. And

58

it still hurts, even now.

When you truly love someone, you learn that they have to be all that really matters. And there was still a wedding to be planned. So the calls went out, and the mad rush to beat the election began. We dove in head-first, together, and within days, we had an officiant, a violinist, and a photographer for our wedding day.

But we still didn't know where we would be getting married. We wanted something outdoors, but in November it often rains in San Francisco, so we had to have a back-up. Then we found the perfect place – a restaurant in the Embarcadero Center, with a beautiful patio overlooking Justin Herman Plaza, the Ferry Building, and the Bay Bridge – a picture-perfect setting for the perfect day. And half the patio was covered, just in case.

As the day drew quickly closer, we watched the weather forecasts diligently. It had been such a dry year – surely, we thought, the odds against rain were high. But as each day passed into the next, the prospects for our sunny, "perfect" day dimmed.

One day, the forecast said 20% rain on our wedding day. 20% in San Francisco in the winter means it might rain, a little, and be sunny, a little, and if you don't like the weather where you're at, just walk a block. On the next, it was 40% – we were worried, but not freaked out. Weather forecasters are wrong all the time, we thought.

Three days out, the odds were up to 60%. We were so glad that we had booked a covered space, but still, no one wants it to rain on their wedding day. Two days, and it topped 80%.

At last, on the day before, as we prepared to drive down to San Francisco once again, rain was a virtual certainty at 100%. And the strongest part of the storm was going to blow through just as we said our vows.

I didn't know whether to be angry or sad, to cry or to laugh.

"It's supposed to be lucky if it rains on your wedding day," Mark said with a grin. So I laughed. And in the end, he was right.

The ceremony started under the tent, as the rain poured down just feet away outside. Mark's mother walked him down the aisle, followed by my mother and me.

I remember so many little, independent things about that afternoon: the violinist playing *The Four Seasons*. The officiant giving us a hurried run-through before, telling us not to forget to breathe, and then stumbling over her words as I leaned over to whisper "breathe" in her ear. My father, reading the piece we chose for him, and telling us it said everything he'd wanted to say to us.

Our mothers together, handing us the candles to light together. Reading each other our vows, and hearing for the first time the words my wonderful partner had chosen to seal his love for me.

The warm, perfect feeling of this is right.

And the rain.

The splattering of the raindrops closed the world in around us, shutting out the traffic, the noise, the rest of the city, until it was just us.

When it was all over, we stood together, alone in each other's arms, and cried.

When we are little, we see people get married on TV, in movies, in real life. Boy meets girl, boy romances girl, and they have the picture-perfect wedding. Growing up as gay kids, as lesbian kids, even as bi- and transgender kids, we dream of that perfect wedding. But we all realized, at some point, that we were never going to have that perfect day, that smiling recognition of our relationships and the affirmation of friends, family, and even our government.

But things can change in an instant, and the impossible can become real.

It was the perfect day. Everyone who was supposed to be there was there, and after 17 years together, though the timing was not what we'd hoped for, it was exactly how it was supposed to be.

Three days later, on November 4, we were at the Obama campaign headquarters in Fair Oaks. We charted candidate Obama's march across the country as he picked up electoral votes in state after state.

Change was in the air. We could all feel it – it was electric. I still remember when he crossed 270 and the cheers went up in the room at the election Barack Obama. I ran outside and called my mom in Tucson to tell her the news. We laughed and we cried, and then we said good night.

Less than an hour later, Prop 8 was passed and slammed the door on marriage equality in California. It was a terrible blow, made all the worse by the contrast with the election of the first African American President in our country's history. It felt like an ending, a painful repudiation of everything we had fought for. Maybe if we had spent more time fighting Prop 8, this wouldn't have happened.

It felt like the end of the world, and although we had gotten married just under the wire once again, we were saddened to think of all the other gay and lesbian couples who were now shut out of what Mark and I shared.

But we were wrong. It wasn't an ending – it was just the beginning.

Still publishing our Marriage Equality Watch news round-up every day, we joined forces with Marriage Equality USA to push for full nationwide same-sex marriage rights.

The pain all of us felt on that November night became a catalyst for a change that would sweep across the country in seven short years, bringing marriage equality to everyone.

We were going to get our revolution, after all. ∞

—

1 You can find Marriage Equality Watch at http://www.purpleunions.com/blog

Equality Is Not a Slogan — It's Our Legal Right

— MICHAEL FARINO

I grew up in a world where we weren't accepted, where I didn't feel complete because I couldn't fully be myself. Many of us had to hide in the closet. So you can imagine why I never thought it possible in my lifetime that marriage would ever be conceivable. "When I get married, or at my wedding," were phrases that were not in my vernacular. It wasn't until our right to marry in California was taken away that I felt provoked to get involved. Not knowing where I could be of service, I decided to fly to California during some of the Proposition 8 hearings and spent a few days outside the courthouse. I remember conversations and arguments with our opposition that brought back desolate feelings of inadequacy and inequality from my childhood. However, some of those conversations gave me a deeper understanding of the imbalance of humanity and the awareness that I had to do something.

Hearing testimony, which was adapted into 8 The Play, cemented my commitment to take action. I was also honored to attend the Prop 8 Gala after-party. Although I traveled by myself, I never felt alone. In attendance were celebrities, many of our peers from the gay community and many of our straight allies. I will never forget chatting with cast members and attendees, all of whom were so approachable and supportive in our quest for equality. I embarked on a journey that until now has been long, yet somehow feels as if it's only just begun. There will always be hate and intolerance, but we must do something different in order to overcome our obstacles. We should learn more about and from our history, because if we don't move forward we will be left behind!

My work, however minor, with MEUSA and MENY, began with rallies,

phone calls, marches and financial support. Too often our acquiescence resulted in compliance to the discrimination and marginalization of our community. New choices needed to be made and MENY gave me the courage to be part of the effort. Even though our beliefs are different from the mainstream, there is enough room for all. Belief is defined as trust, faith, or confidence in someone or something. Equality is defined as a symbolic expression of the fact that two quantities are equal, as in an equation. In the 1980s I watched our brothers and sisters die, and was powerless. MENY gave us all the courage and support to say, "No more! This is our time!" Despite our differences, we are inherently the same in that we are all part of one human race, all having a human experience; and we all want to be loved and respected. This is our chance to show the world that we may love differently but that #loveislove! I am indebted to everyone at MEUSA and those all around the globe who have worked diligently toward the larger and necessary goal of legal rights and equality for everyone. I am honored and deeply thankful to be part of the marriage equality community, and I am eagerly hopeful for a future of non-discrimination where we are all truly equal. ∞

Equality Is Not a Slogan — It's Our Legal Right

MICHAEL FARINO

On the Road to Equality Nationwide

– STUART GAFFNEY & JOHN LEWIS

We always know where to go in San Francisco when something big – good
or bad – happens for the LGBT community: the corner of Castro and Market
Streets. When we heard the news on November 18, 2003 that the Massachusetts
Supreme Court had just ruled in favor of marriage equality, we made sure we
were at that historic street corner at 5:00 p.m.

When we arrived, we witnessed something that we had never quite seen
before: an amazingly articulate woman addressing the crowd, megaphone in
hand, wearing of all things a white wedding dress. We asked ourselves, who
is that incredible woman in a wedding dress? We soon learned it was Molly
McKay, one of the leaders of Marriage Equality California (MECA), a precursor
to Marriage Equality USA (MEUSA). Many other pioneering marriage equality activists and leaders, including her future wife Davina Kotulski, were also
on stage, and they spoke powerfully about why the right to marry was fundamental. Together for 16 years at that point, we had already decided we wanted
to get involved in the burgeoning marriage equality movement. We knew at
that moment that we wanted to start working with these inspiring activists. We
soon found out that Marriage Equality would be holding another rally – this
time on the steps of San Francisco City Hall on National Freedom to Marry
Day, February 12, 2004.

We planned for John to join the February 12 rally and then report back
that evening to Stuart, who had to be at work all day. When John arrived at the
rally, he spotted Molly in her signature wedding dress, and asked her about
the plans for the rally. Her response was extraordinary: "You can walk right
into San Francisco City Hall and get married." What? What?! WHAT?! John

64

couldn't believe his ears. San Francisco Mayor Gavin Newsom had just decided to stop discriminating against LGBT couples and open the doors of City Hall to all loving, committed couples to marry. We could get married – right then. Only one problem ... no Stuart. Neither of us owned cell phones, but John, in a stroke of luck caught Stuart at his desk, just before he went to lunch. Instead of having lunch, he dashed to join John at City Hall where we were astonished to become one of the first ten couples to get married.

When we heard the words "by virtue of the authority vested in me by the State of California, I now pronounce you spouses for life," we felt something transform within us. For the first time, we experienced our government treating us as fully equal human beings as gay people and recognizing us as a loving couple worthy of the full respect of the law. The experience was so transformative that we committed to do everything in our power to make the freedom to marry – and most importantly, the respect and dignity that comes with it – available to all.

February 12, 2004 was the first day of what became known as San Francisco's "Winter of Love," a month in which over 4,000 LGBT couples from 46 states and eight countries came to the city to get married. We took part and got married because of Marriage Equality USA.

Later that year, the California Supreme Court invalidated the marriages because it ruled that the courts needed to decide whether the state constitution mandated marriage equality before San Francisco could marry same-sex couples. However, the Winter of Love unleashed irrepressible excitement, inspiration, and dedication for nationwide marriage equality unlike anything seen before. Once you've tasted equality and had it taken away, you have to get it back.

Later in 2004, Marriage Equality California activists, led by Davina Kotulski, decided to channel this seemingly boundless energy into a nationwide bus tour – the Marriage Equality Express – nicknamed "the caravan." The purpose of the caravan was to "share the love" – and more concretely to give people across our nation the opportunity to meet LGBT couples, their friends, and family, to see our common humanity, and to hear our real life stories of how marriage discrimination harms real people.

The 44 caravan riders included San Francisco newlyweds; bi-national couples, whose relationships and families were torn apart or threatened because of unfair immigration laws that were part of the misnamed "Defense of Marriage Act"; military veteran couples who had served under the burden of Don't Ask, Don't Tell; parents of LGBT people; children of LGBT couples; and ministers. The group was racially diverse, with African Americans, Latinos, Asian Americans, and mixed race Americans all playing active and visible roles. We were thrilled to join the caravan.

The caravan's stops across the country varied widely. We joined local activists to conduct rallies all across the country in places as varied as Laramie, Denver, St. Louis, Akron, Pittsburgh and more. In Washington DC, we put on the first national marriage equality rally. The national rally featured personal stories from all of the caravan's riders and speeches by DC Congressional delegate and civil rights legend Eleanor Holmes Norton and California State Senator Mark Leno.

We also participated in local community events in Cheyenne, Wyoming; Indianapolis, Indiana; and Columbus, Ohio. One unusual stop was at the Silver Bells Wedding Chapel in Reno, Nevada, where same-sex couples from the caravan, fully dressed in wedding attire, asked to get married. After the somewhat stunned receptionist declined the request, we switched partners so that we were different sex couples, and asked if the chapel could marry us. She responded they could. We explained that although we were friends with our new "partners," we had years-long, loving, committed relationships with our real partners. The event illuminated the arbitrariness and absurdity of these exclusionary laws – and made front page news.

Everywhere we went, we utilized the media. The San Francisco Chronicle dispatched a reporter and photographer to travel with us and ran daily reports from the caravan. The caravan was usually the lead story on the local television news wherever we went. Even when there were small crowds for events, the local news stations and newspapers came out, enabling us to further our goal of putting a human face of the issue. C-SPAN 2 broadcast the entire rally nationwide.

When we embarked on the caravan, none of the states on the itinerary had marriage equality. Now a dozen years later, LGBT couples can marry everywhere the Marriage Equality Express rolled into town – indeed in every state in the union. Marriage Equality USA's focus on telling the stories and sharing the hopes and dreams of LGBT people with the nation was integral to this victory. We have confidence that the journey that the caravan and Marriage Equality USA traveled will continue to inspire others along the road to full nationwide equality in all aspects of our lives. ∞

On the Road to Equality Nationwide

STUART GAFFNEY
& JOHN LEWIS

Homophobia: *noun*
ho·mo·pho·bia \ hō-mə-fō-bē-ə\

— TIM GARCIA

Picture it: the first anniversary of the narrow but successful passage of California's Proposition 8. A shopping center corner at the busy intersection of a rural town during the evening rush hour. A handful of Marriage Equality USA members proudly donning organizational logos and attire, some holding large posters and lit candles. Suddenly, without warning: guttural laughter. Honking. "Faggots!" Screeching tires. "Yes On 8!" Speeding vehicles veering alarmingly close. "YES ON 8!" More muffled jeering. Then again, with burning zeal: "FAGGOTS!!" The swelling hatred in the feverish shrieks was brutally visceral, shrill, and almost animalistic. Without laying a finger on any of us the piercing vitriol of passersby made my blood run cold, filling my body with fight-or-flight adrenaline and triggering overwhelming waves of fear, vulnerability and a dizzying panic.

Instead of retreating back to my car to calm my wobbly legs and catch my breath, instead of surrendering to rabid intimidation and recoiling into seclusion, I took a deep breath and a (figurative and literal) step forward on the corner of that busy intersection. An unprecedented and tenacious drive stirred within me – part anger, part sadness, and an increasingly clear realization that what we were facing must be part of something much more significant than a civil marriage ceremony and certificate.

Over the next few weeks a loud internal dialogue was waged. Standing on that intersection opened a floodgate of pent-up emotion stemming from ferocious bullying I experienced as a young boy. I desperately yearned for answers. I wanted to make sense of everything. WHERE did this condemnatory fervor come from? WHAT drove complete strangers to unleash such malicious threats and assaults? None of it made sense. Was there really something wrong with me? Wiping away the tears, I soon found myself reading analogous definitions of one particular word.

Homophobia: noun ho·mo·pho·bia \hō-mə-fō-bē-ə\ the irrational fear of, aversion to, or discrimination against, homosexuality and homosexuals; unreasoning fear of, or antipathy toward, homosexuals and homosexuality. First known use: 1969.

THIS was my "Ah-Ha" moment: I, we, were all up against something inherently irrational (a baseless fear manifested as hate), and in order to effectively battle this historically deceptive and insidious mentality (think back to Anita Bryant's Save Our Children campaign and the Briggs Initiatives' parallels to Yes on 8's Protect Our Children), we needed brave visibility. And standing on that corner was just that.

Moreover, for the first time in my young life, I interpreted the fight for marriage equality as more than a talking point and partisan issue within the prevailing political arena. It was also a movement that transcended relationship statuses. The important work being done resonated on much more profound levels to ALL of us (partnered LGBT people who longed to marry AND single LGBT people). It was a battle to establish, affirm and uphold our humanity. It was a new platform for an age-old standoff between the pervasive social toxicity, that is homophobia, and those of us wanting to expose and ultimately delegitimize these irrational forces of intolerance.

Soon after connecting the dots, so to speak, I began to hold my head up a little higher at subsequent rallies and events, and as I lived my life in general, particularly when confronted by homophobic opposition and their thinly-veiled discriminatory rhetoric (think "One Man + One Woman"). Not only did I habitually remind myself that truth and rationality were on our side, but I had a firmer grasp of what was at stake: not just civil marriage licenses for the engaged and prospective newlyweds, but our very lives. Most importantly the lives of all young LGBT people who, on a daily basis, are enduring the same type of harmful and illogically based viciousness unleashed on that busy intersection. ∞

Homophobia:
noun
ho·mo·pho·bia
\hō-mə-fō-bē-ə

TIM GARCIA

Gender Offenders Are Brides Gone Wild!

– GENDER OFFENDERS

In 2007, Candy Samples (Will Harrell), Chic (Michael Cavazos) and Sassy Parker, came together with director Brian Maschka to create a work that would speak out against traditional ideas of marriage and raise questions about its sanctity, gender roles, and equality. Together, we were known as the political sketch comedy troupe, Gender Offenders. Inspired by our involvement with Marriage Equality New York (MENY), we created the show Brides Gone Wild! to speak in favor of equality.

Gender Offenders was formed the previous year in 2006. Candy, Chic and Sassy are three drag queens from different parts of the country who had the shared experience of growing up sissy and attending the same performing arts program at Emerson College. Using our theatre background was the best way we knew how to voice our political concerns and found that audiences more easily considered and examined societal issues best when served to them through comedy and song.

Our relationship with MENY began through friends in New York City and specifically in our neighborhood of Astoria, Queens. We were fortunate enough to have some members of MENY attend one of our early Christmas shows, Jingle Balls and Mistle-hos. Understanding our point of view, they became fans and would ask us to host The Wedding March rally in 2007. We were thrilled and excited to be asked, but the question remained, "How can three theatre queens help with the marriage equality movement?" One might believe that a 21st century civil rights movement would consist of a much more subdued political crowd, the skirts and suits type, wouldn't it? Having grown up effeminate, we had already grown accustomed to fighting and defending ourselves. Our

70

art was just a reflection of our experience. We had no idea how timely and how greatly our ideas would resonate with audiences. History at that point had rarely shown people like us fighting for rights so we were not sure if we had the stuff of great activists like Harvey Milk, Larry Kramer, Barney Frank or Christine Quinn. Yes, we were established drag performers that provided entertainment to marches and Pride events, but we soon learned that we were a lot more than that. We were representatives of a drag community that had previously been pushed into the shadows and who were also becoming outspoken advocates, activists and leaders. Our little drag troupe found its voice and, with the support of MENY's Cathy Marino-Thomas and Ron Zacchi, we were able to speak to audiences through art. Instead of bullhorns and chants, we created music and soundscapes, instead of speeches we raised questions through stage dialogue and physical comedy, and instead of protest signs, we used our faces and bodies as canvas. We graciously accepted the invitation to host the rally and helped organize a group of LGBTQ artists and allies to perform, including comedian Allison Castillo, dancer Jeffrey Peterson, drag performer Diamond Dunhill, and singer/songwriter Robert German, among others.

Shorty after receiving the invitation, we began brainstorming ideas for our next show. We took on the theme of marriage to discuss the "tradition" – holy and otherwise – of heterosexual marriage, questioning the hypocrisy found in "traditional" ideas of what marriage is "supposed" to be. Brian Maschka would serve as a dramaturge and director, working to shape the show's story arc, to find the humor and relevancy in our writing, and to bring Brides Gone Wild! to life. The show was also successful due to the talents of costume designer Alan Parker, photographer Rachel Watson, and pianist Jeff Cubeta.

Brides Gone Wild! opened with a wedding ceremony, between Chic and Sassy, dressed in wedding attire. After a traditional wedding procession, Candy, dressed as a member of the clergy, began officiating the marriage. She said, "Dearly beloved, we are gathered here today on this beautiful Saturday evening to join these two women in holy matrimony." But before she could proceed a loud police siren and bullhorn was heard and the voice of "the law" shouted, "Not in this town! Same-sex marriage is against nature, against God and, mostly, against the law!" We Gender Offenders shouted in return and refused to back down. Instead, we sang our opening number, the title song, which included the following lyrics: Who's to say our love's wrong or right?/ Who's to say how we live our own life?/And now we're ready, armed and riled/ We're brides gone wild!/This protest has been filed/We're brides gone wild!

The show continued with scenes including "Lucy Roberts," a commercial for a gym's bridal boot camp that lampooned the extremes some brides go through to lose weight before their big day. "The Bridezilla," which offered commentary on obsessive, controlling brides who, forgetting the true meaning of a wedding day, become monsters only concerned with appearances. There was an infomercial called "Vaginoplasty" which took on the idea of a "white wedding" and what to do when you are no longer a virgin bride. There was a '50s television style scene called "Normal Not Normal," that explored the relationship between two young girls and their families. Cindy has two mothers while Jennifer has a mother and father. How does this affect their family dynamics and the morality of these two girls? We also debated the authenticity of things like mail-order brides in a song called "American Wife" and contemporary American wedding rituals through a talk show sketch called "The Rear View."

A few days before the show opened, we ventured into the city to conduct our own social experiment and to delve deeper into heterosexual bridal traditions by having a "real" bachelorette party. We bounced around from bar to bar, playing games from a bachelorette party game book that included ideas for a sort of scavenger hunt. We asked people frivolous questions and collected items like pictures, drinks and men's underwear. It was a very silly tradition that we each had little to no experience with before that night. It was still only 2007, before we had legal marriage in the state of New York. Yet, as we went from one venue to the next and explained to people we were having a bachelorette party, we found that most people wanted to join in our fun. They participated in our quizzes and took interest in our show and the fight for marriage equality. Even though it was not a real bachelorette party, people took it seriously. It was real that night. Now, in 2016 as we write this, those things can happen in the LGBTQ community. That tradition, silly as it may seem to some, is no longer exclusive to our heterosexual counterparts.

The show concluded with a musical number called, "Catch the Bouquet!" by the Gender Offenders' alter egos, The Corsettes. Dressed in the tradition of a '60s all girl group in matching outfits, The Corsettes harken back to an earlier time when the Civil Rights Movement was just beginning. Martin Luther King, Jr. proclaimed his famous I Have a Dream speech in 1963. In 2007, over 40 years later, The Corsettes sang out about their dream of equal rights, and, in the song, they proclaim that the next marriage would be for us, the LGBTQ community. It included the following lyrics and rap:

> *I've waited so long/patiently so long/but tonight's gonna be the night/ Nothing can go wrong/cause now I'm so strong/and I'll use all my might/ I'm feeling lucky/I believe in fate/and the tide is gonna turn/Don't try and stop me/Girl, don't hate/or you'll really feel my burn/I'm gonna catch, catch/catch the bouquet/I'm the next to wear that gown/I'm gonna catch, catch/catch the bouquet/I'm gonna tear up this town ... Now's the time/ we got to get in line/Here's the story/morning glory/It's my time to shine/ Don't you protest/I'm gonna show my pride/Always a bride's maid/and never a bride/I want a pimped out groom/standing by my side/slip the ring on my finger/marriage state of mind/we gotta fight for our right/to wedded bliss/look out boyfriend/here comes a same-sex kiss/Do you catch, catch, catch my drift/we want our civil rights/or else we're gonna get pissed/I may not be able to catch a football play/but when the smoke clears/I will have caught the bouquet.*

Brides Gone Wild! played two sold out weekends at The Duplex right in the heart of Greenwich Village. We are so proud to have been able to contribute to the fight through our own medium. Our work with MENY was just beginning, though. We would go on to march the entire length of the pride parade that year in wedding dresses and heels. We also participated in Queens Pride, hosted The Wedding March rally in 2008, and continued to attend and perform at various events throughout the years since joining MENY's fight in 2007.

Our fore-drag mothers, like Marsha P. Johnson and Sylvia Rivera, were great leaders who remind us that everyone has a voice, everyone can promote change, and everyone has a home somewhere on that rainbow flag. Today, armed with the lessons we learned from working with MENY, we continue to advocate for transgender justice, racial equality and HIV/AIDS activism and education. Gender Offenders are proud to be the daughters of Stonewall and to have contributed to the fight for equal rights. ∞

I Want to Lead a Gay Pride Parade

— MIKE GOETTEMOELLER

Before starting a new job on Wall Street, I asked my Mom if she'd like to do a trip with me to California — a drive from San Francisco to Los Angeles. I lived in the San Francisco Bay area for many years and had friendships up and down the coast. Mom, while enjoying her recent visits to my current home in New York City, jumped at the chance to visit a state she used to imagine herself living in during her younger years.

During our family's Easter festivities in Ohio the day before our trip, my oldest sister was surprised to hear of our plans and jokingly thanked me for the invite. I quickly checked my frequent flier accounts and quipped, "I can get you on the 4:00 p.m. flight tomorrow to SFO, let me know." Mom and I had a new travel partner.

Wine tastings in Sonoma, lounging around foggy San Francisco, hyperbole drive down the I-5 through the Central Valley, dinner in Malibu, stroll through the Hollywood Walk of Fame, time spent with friends in Manhattan Beach and of course, shopping — it was quite the memorable trip. During the last evening of our adventure, Mom and my sister were having a conversation as I was on my laptop taking care of a few administrative items for my new job. Out of their chatter, I heard my sister ask our Mom, who she was joking with about turning 80 in a few months, what was left on her bucket list. To my sister's surprise Mom belted, "I want to lead a gay pride parade." Without skipping a beat I piped in, "I can make it happen, let me know!" I went about my work and nothing more was said. The position on top of her bucket list did not overly surprise me given she has become quite the LGBTQ advocate over the years, though I dismissed it as her just trying to get a reaction out of my sister.

A few weeks later, memories of our trip fading, I received a phone call from Mom inquiring about marching in a parade. She thought Columbus, OH would be fun (and I am sure it would be), but I mentioned if she was going to do it, do it right – come to NYC! It was the eve of the Supreme Court decision on marriage equality and regardless of the outcome, the parade, across the nation, would have great significance. She called me the next day letting me know her and my youngest sister would be attending.

I quickly called my friend Brian Silva, who was the Executive Director at Marriage Equality USA, asking if it was OK for the three of us to march. Of course it was. On the day of the parade, we lined up early where Mom quickly went about making friends with many of the participants – hearing their stories and sharing ours. My Mom, having now passed 80, couldn't walk the entire two-mile route, so I pushed her in a wheelchair. Once we started the parade route, the energy was electric. Almost three million people, lined up on both sides of the street, there to cheer us on. Mom was not content with merely getting a ride down the middle of the road, but wanted to connect with the spectators. We hugged the side of the parade route for Mom to hand out stickers. Instead of merely passing them out, Mom held each recipient's hands for ever so briefly a moment. I am not sure the impact Mom had on the crowd that day, but to those spectators who held my Mom's hands, you have affected her for life. My sister mentioned that during several moments of the parade, Mom had tears roll down her face. Whether they were tears released from recalling the difficulties we faced together during my coming-out years, the realization that we're not alone and have a voice, from the joy of all the beautiful people in attendance, or some combination of the above, I want to thank Marriage Equality USA for making my Mom's dream (and millions of others, including me) a reality. ∞

There Are Gay People Everywhere: the Fight for Marriage Equality in California's Central Valley

– BALTIMORE GONZALEZ

My husband Robert and I were married on March 11, 2001. We had been introduced to each other by mutual friends at a restaurant, and that evening we made an emotional connection that neither of us expected. After spending some time together in the days to come, Robert and I felt we were kindred spirits. We were both Taurus's with very strong personalities! We both had a similar familial background and both were a bit conservative, having grown up in small towns. I was born and raised in Madera, California, and Robert is from Willows, in Northern California.

I was raised Catholic and attended church regularly growing up. I didn't think it was fair to place doubt in the minds of LGBT people as to whether or not God accepted them. I consider myself to be a very spiritual person; however, I do not attend a particular church regularly. Friends and family always say I am one of the most spiritual people they know. I was never going to allow anyone to take that from me. My relationship with my Higher Power was much too strong to have hatred come between me and that Power. I always believed in my heart that the God that I believed in created me in his image and I was exactly who I was supposed to be.

My experience had always been standing up for the rights of others, not my own. My authentic self was something that I took pride in. I have never been ashamed of who I am. I was, however, not accustomed to being in front of news crews speaking of my personal life and taking the risk that in the very conservative town of Fresno, California, something might happen to me. Since I had always stood up for others and the injustices towards others, I felt it was time I stood up for something that personally affected me.

There Are Gay
le Everywhere:
the Fight for
rriage Equality
in California's
Central Valley

BALTIMORE
GONZALEZ

At that time, I would never have imagined that one day I would be speaking in front of the California State Assembly committee, personally invited by California legislator and marriage equality advocate Mark Leno, or going before the Fresno City Council and the Fresno Board of Supervisors and asking them to proclaim National Coming Out Day. I never thought I would stand with the person I loved at the County Clerk's office to ask for a marriage license that I knew would be rejected. All of these happened after I became the Volunteer Chapter Leader for Marriage Equality California (MECA, which became a chapter of Marriage Equality USA/MEUSA in 2006) and for Equality California in Fresno, California in 2004. All in the name of love!

I have bittersweet memories of my part in the fight for marriage equality: Being one of the very last couples to say our vows in the 2004 San Francisco Winter of Love before someone came screaming through the beautiful San Francisco City Hall yelling, "Go get your paper's signed, they just put a halt on the marriages," was one of the most surreal experiences in my life. Taking on the Mayor of Fresno, Alan Autry, after he endorsed and promoted a "Heterosexual Marriage Celebration" in front of Fresno City Hall. (After threatening a lawsuit, we were granted a "Gay Marriage Celebration" with the same amenities that were granted to them.) And testifying before the California State Assembly. The day after the Assembly hearing I read this in newspapers from all over the U.S., "There are gay people everywhere," Gonzales said. "This is not going to go away."

One weekend during my marriage equality work, I received a phone call asking if my husband, Robert, and I would "recreate," if you will, our marriage experience. The part came for us to give each other a kiss. I was assured this would air only once. The next thing I knew it was airing over and over again. However, I was not out to my parents. I called and pleaded with the cable company to shut off my parent's cable temporarily. The gentleman who worked for the cable company said to me, "Baltimore, maybe it's time you told your father?" Although I thought his idea was genius, I wasn't ready to have that sit-down just yet, nor have I to this day. It's a "Don't ask, Don't tell" situation. My father and I have a great relationship where I do not discuss my personal relationships with him and I am okay with that. Family is very important to me, and I cherish the relationship we have just the way it is for now.

The bitter aspect of this fight was reckoning with the fact that all the love I and others were trying to share and evoke in people sometimes seemed to be backfiring. I had clergy, regular citizens, professionals, and Christians yelling derogatory names at me all too frequently. I had my life threatened over and over again. I gave a speech at Fresno City Hall where I was assigned two armed undercover police officers who stood by my side in case someone tried to shoot me.

These were things that were happening behind the scenes, that my family and the general public were not aware of. I was seen by people either as a hero or as someone they loathed! It was very difficult never knowing who was on my side.

Eventually, I decided to hand the marriage equality baton over to someone else after I lost my trust for the media. I felt justified in stepping back in that I'd put as much effort and energy into the fight for marriage equality as I could handle. I had been receiving so many death threats that they had become a normal part of life, and watching my back everywhere I went had become tiresome. On the other hand, nothing will ever replace the feeling of when a stranger walked up to me and asked for a hug, an autograph, or just simply wanted to say, "Thank you for all that you're doing!"

I couldn't begin to imagine all of this not being part of my life. I am proud of the work I put into the fight and of all the hard work others put into it. What I accomplished was worth every single time I cried after a protest, rally, or celebration where I'd been called everything but my name. I will always value my experiences and the opportunity I had to be part of creating history. ∞

There Are Gay
People Everyw
the Fight for
Marriage Equa
in California's
Central Valley

BALTIMORE
GONZALEZ

Our Red Cape Campaign

— TRACY HOLLISTER

A red cape remains the most vivid of many fond memories from my year and-a-half on staff at Marriage Equality USA (MEUSA). Our volunteers donned this red cape after they made calls for the "Freedom Indiana" campaign from our New York City-based call center. Other volunteers and I were delighted to watch each volunteer stretch their arms before them with the cape billowing behind them as they "flew" around our conference table, one at a time. Another volunteer blasted the Superman theme song from his iPhone and speakers, giving the volunteers further dramatic license to take on the role of Superman. It is why we used the red cape and how it lifted our volunteers up during this difficult campaign that makes me smile.

I used this red cape in my capacity as Field Director for MEUSA's National Equality Action Team (NEAT). Through both our virtual and in-person phone banks, NEAT brought out-of-state volunteer resources across the country to complement states' marriage campaigns. Our Executive Director Brian Silva started NEAT to help win four marriage-related ballot initiatives in November 2012. In fact, it was because of how inspired I was after witnessing these victories just six months after I experienced our country's last of about 30 "straight" ballot box losses in North Carolina that I joined MEUSA in the first place. I wanted to be a part of the national momentum.

With NEAT, I was responsible for recruiting volunteers, orienting them to the campaign, and doing what we could to retain them by ensuring that their experience was meaningful and rewarding. When I arrived in New York City in May 2013, I was lucky to inherit an experienced core team, recruiting and confirmation processes, and training materials. Retention was important

80

because it was hard to find people willing to phone bank in the first place. Most people are repelled by the idea of calling strangers about one of our country's most polarizing topics. Once they got there, those who stuck with it for repeat phone banking were the heart and soul of our work; their willingness to devote their time and energy to these campaigns was critical to our success. If any experienced volunteer left, it would take a while to find and train another. In fact, when thinking about the collective contribution of each of our small groups of loyal phone bankers in each location, I often thought of this quote by Margaret Meade: "Never doubt that a small group of thoughtful, committed citizens can change the world. Indeed, it is the only thing that ever has."

The key was maintaining that commitment. Truth be told, phone banking is not easy. Volunteers sometimes wait several minutes before the automated calling system finds them a live person. Once the volunteer speaks, that person might hang up – or make judgmental or hurtful comments such as:

> *"Gays are disgusting perverts. They should not have any rights." "I believe in what the Bible says. It's a sin to be gay. They are going to hell." "I just don't think we should mess with God's definition of marriage. Marriage is between a man and a woman. Period." "Marriage is about children. I do not think homosexuals should be raising children."*

Occasional in most other campaigns, such comments seemed to be more frequent in the Indiana campaign. Fortunately, nearly all of the volunteers who helped with NYC's phone banks for Indiana were veteran phone bankers who had worked on other marriage campaigns. They knew to expect such comments and how to handle them. They were trained not to argue back but to be polite, thanking opponents for their time and moving on to the next call. Yet even our most seasoned volunteers – most of whom were lesbian or gay themselves – would not be human if such comments did not get to us in some way. Certain comments might even trigger traumatic memories with family members or friends.

After a few Indiana phone banks in our Times Square (NYC) call center, I saw, heard and felt the exasperation of our volunteers. Our usually resilient crew was more ragged and discouraged.

Why was the "Freedom Indiana" campaign more difficult? Ironically, the same factors that made it strategically smart and effective were the things that made it take a stronger emotional toll.

First, we were fighting against more than an anti-marriage equality amendment. In its second sentence, Indiana's amendment was also an anti-LGBT relationship recognition amendment that forbade things like civil unions. HJR-3 stated: "Only marriage between one man and one woman shall be valid or recognized as a marriage in Indiana. A legal status identical or substantially similar to that of marriage for unmarried individuals shall not be valid or recognized."

In Indiana our goal was not to find "Hoosiers" (citizens of Indiana) who supported marriage equality, but rather find voters who felt the second part of the amendment went too far. To me, it felt as if we as callers and they as voters were essentially saying: "I understand outlawing full marriage equality. But to outlaw anything similar to marriage like civil unions? That is just too harsh and extreme!" To many of us at NEAT this messaging tactic, while strategically necessary, was a difficult pill to swallow. We were convinced that only marriage allowed for full equality, while civil unions were separate and inherently unequal. But in a state where most people were against marriage for same-sex couples, it was easier to find more who supported civil unions and would oppose the amendment for that reason.

Besides, the goal was not to have the legislature completely defeat the entire anti-marriage equality amendment but to have legislators amend part of the amendment. In Indiana, the exact proposed constitutional amendments had to be passed by two consecutive general assemblies. HJR-3 had been passed by a previous legislature in its two-sentence format and needed to be passed exactly that way to get on the ballot. But, if we could get legislators to change any of the wording or drop the second sentence, we would prevent the amendment from getting on the November 2014 ballot. By the time any revised amendment came before the second Indiana General Assembly again, the campaign leaders wisely reasoned, it very well might be a moot point. The momentum toward marriage equality was moving fast. The Supreme Court of the United States might have then have ruled (as it in fact did in June 2015) in favor of full marriage equality for all 50 states – settling the matter for the whole country.

Personally, the Indiana amendment brought back bad memories for me. In banning civil unions, it was one of the more extreme types of anti-marriage equality amendments like the one I'd seen pass in North Carolina less than two years earlier. I poured my heart into defeating NC's amendment, running 33 of the state's largest phone banks and resigning from my full-time job to volunteer to try and defeat it. But we lost, and it was devastating. In North Carolina, too, we had painful messaging. We spoke about the "unintended consequences" of Amendment One, or how it would hurt unmarried straight people – as if the "intended consequences" to ban gay couples from marrying were somehow okay. What if, I thought, our efforts at NEAT could help prevent LGBT Hoosiers from going through the same collective and months-long hassle we endured in North Carolina?

The final thing that made Indiana more difficult was the focus on getting the highest number of conservatives to leave voicemails for legislators. Why? Because, like North Carolina, the Indiana General Assembly had a supermajority of Republicans, so the campaign leaders felt they would be more responsive to (or less dismissive of) messages from fellow conservative voters. This strategy meant that we were less likely to be talking with someone who was sympathetic toward LGBT people and more likely to receive difficult comments. Again, while strategic, this was more challenging – if not intimidating – for our volunteers as voters sometimes shared their prejudices with us, often not knowing that they were speaking with an LGBT person.

To overcome these challenges, I asked myself, "How do we keep this loyal group of volunteers coming back? How do we lift their spirits and show them how important their efforts are?" One weekend, while walking in my Brooklyn neighborhood with one of our volunteer trainers, Andrew Zibell, the answer became clear.

My eyes lit up as we walked by the window of the Brooklyn Superhero Supply

Store. I was tickled at how "campy" the store was. Inside, they sold empty but meaningful gallon-size paint-can-like tins of attributes like Chutzpuh and Magnificence. We bought a little canister of Justice and a hand-held gadget that lit up and made loud pulsing buzzing sounds that I later called the "Inoculator." I decided to use this before our volunteers got on the call center floor to inoculate them against all sorts of rudeness, verbal abuse, or negativity they might encounter. And then we saw it — the thing that could really make a difference to our volunteers: a red cape.

Giddy with excitement, Andrew and I planned that each volunteer was to wear the cape and be applauded for their Superman-like feats of phone banking during this campaign. Although many of our volunteers expressed an initial reluctance to do this silly act, they grew emboldened when I and the other volunteers goaded them on. Once each of our ten or so core volunteers had the courage to allow me to tie a red cape around their necks, they then found themselves smiling or giggling as they ran around our conference table, embracing their own inner hero.

Fortunately, the red cape had the intended effect: bringing lightness and laughter, lifting our spirits, retaining our volunteers, and celebrating our collective heroism in enduring painful conversations. They were doing the important and necessary but difficult work to keep our national momentum to win marriage equality going, state by state, call by call, difficult conversation after difficult conversation.

And in the end, Freedom Indiana's campaign strategy worked, and enough legislators voted to remove the "extreme" second sentence. This prevented the anti-marriage equality amendment from going before the voters of Indiana.

It's impossible to say whether it was NEAT volunteers who made the critical difference in winning Indiana's campaign in the legislature. Perhaps if we had not been a part of the campaign, the amendment would have passed the legislature and passed at the ballot box; then, Indiana might have stopped the country's sense that winning marriage equality was inevitable. But we can say that our volunteers were super men and women who answered the call of justice and made a difference. They all deserved to wear that red cape. ∞

We Are Not Going to Leave

— MARK "MAJOR" JIMINEZ & BEAU CHANDLER

On July 5, 2012, we went to the Records building in Dallas, TX and applied for a marriage license. The day after Independence Day was not a random choice, as we both felt it was time for ALL Texans to be free from unjust laws and Constitutional Amendments which denied us the right to be married.

We applied for our marriage license electronically and then waited in line to be called upon by one of the clerks. When she did call our names, and it was determined that we were both of the same sex, we were informed that Texas law prevented them from issuing us a marriage license and we were denied.

When we were denied our marriage license, we handcuffed ourselves together and said that we were not going to leave until they gave us our license. We then sat down and blocked the line to the counter where couples go to obtain their marriage licenses. Each time one of the clerks said "Next!" we politely, but firmly, informed them that we, indeed, were next in line. They choose to ignore that and just moved the line around us so that every single couple behind us could get their marriage licenses and be on their way to a happy life together as a married couple.

We stayed put the entire afternoon, handcuffed together, until they closed. At closing time we were told to leave. We informed them that we had been waiting all afternoon for our license and that we had been passed over and denied just for being who we are. We again reiterated that we were not going to leave without a marriage license. We stayed put. We then were arrested and taken to jail. We were both charged with Criminal Trespass. ∞

left–right

Our booking pictu
Mark "Major" Jimi
and Beau Chandle

Waiting it out.

85

A Day in the Life of a Love Warrior

— DAVINA KOTULSKI, PH.D.

August 13, 2010. I got up at 4:00 a.m. today, dressed quickly in a black suit, and drove in darkness to San Francisco City Hall with my wife, Molly McKay. No breakfast, no coffee, just the excitement of Judge Walker's impending ruling regarding the Prop 8 stay to chew on.

We were so cold when we got out of the car. It was the San Francisco summer cold that Mark Twain joked about, bone-chilling cold with fog and drizzle. We approached the reporters who had asked us to come down for a live 5:00 a.m. interview. I might have suggested an 8:00 a.m. or 7:00 a.m. compromise, but I knew Molly was going with or without me.

When we arrived, fellow Marriage Equality USA advocates, Kristin and Teresa who hoped they'd be able to legally marry if Judge Walker lifted the stay, had risen even earlier and driven even farther, and were already there shivering as they spoke live to an early morning audience about why they wanted to be legally married.

Last May, Kristin was taken to the ER in Fresno after suffering repeated grand mal seizures in the sweltering heat at the Meet in the Middle Event. Hospital staff denied Teresa the right to be with Kristin, (even though she had medical power of attorney), and they refused to listen to her when she told them what meds not to give Kristin. And as you might expect they gave Kristin meds she was not supposed to have and her condition worsened. Kristin and Teresa never want to go through that again, so they were going to be the first in line to get their marriage license.

Did I mention it was cold? We shivered and waited for the sun to rise, then moved from the Civic Center Plaza to the steps of San Francisco City Hall.

Same-sex couples began lining up to get their marriage licenses.

Then the opposition, all five of them, began showing up. At first Molly thought two of them were a same-sex couple who were there to get married. Is it surprising that two of the guys Luke and Victor are handsome, kinda beefy, and well-dressed? Hmm. Anyway, they brought their gigantic anti-gay billboard signs "Pervert Judge, Pervert Ruling." "A moral wrong is not a civil right." "Judge Mocks God." The usual. And they took their places in front of SF City Hall steps.

9:00 a.m. came quickly and we waited for Judge Walker's decision. More cameras, more photographers, more interviews, more same-sex couples showing up, more people gathering.

10:00 a.m. crowd grows.

11:00 a.m. crowd grows impatient.

What the heck? Where is this decision? Why is he torturing us and waiting until the last minute?

The fog suddenly lifts and now we are way too hot in our extra layers of clothes. My face begins to burn almost instantly. The reporters press in closer and there is so much body heat. Molly jokes about taking bets of what time the judge might make his decision. 11:01, 11:08, 11:31, 11:55.

As the minutes tick by, the media presses even closer, surrounding Molly and me and the two same-sex couples, Teresa and Kristin, and Vanessa and Maria. We are pushed up against the City Hall wall, unable to turn without bumping someone's camera lens.

No one is winning this bet. It's now 12:00 p.m. Where is this decision? Some people in the crowd who we can't see over the video equipment and cameras are cheering. Turns out it's just a tourist bus going by. People, focus!

Then someone gets a Facebook message and another a Tweet. The Judge has lifted the stay, they say. "Source, source, source?" we yell. But no one has a reliable source. We call our sources. They've heard nothing.

The media are hungry. We are like cornered animals against the wall and the media are hungry predators seeking morsels of news, their lips smacking for word. A cheer goes out to my left. It's not the tourist bus this time.

A Day in the
Life of a
Love Warrior

DAVINA
KOTULSKI, PH.D.

"Source, source, source?" we ask again. "Lambda Legal," someone yells out. We cheer. We applaud, but something doesn't feel right. We give the reporters the happy faces they came for. Then we rush into City Hall with our friends who want marriage licenses.

There are 40 couples ready for this day, beaming and shaking in anticipation of making it legal. I race up and down the line snapping photos and congratulating them.

And that nagging feeling returns. I call Pamela Brown, Marriage Equality USA's policy director. She still does not have a source. I look for someone from City Hall. They have a concerned look on their face. He did say to lift the stay, but something isn't plain.

Then Pamela tells me. "The stay will be kept in place until August 18."

There will be no weddings today.

The hallway is jam-packed with happy couples along the right side of the wall and throngs of reporters on the left. There is barely an aisle for people to walk down.

Word is starting to be blurted out. It's going to get really chaotic. It needs to be a clean delivery, not a drawn out wave of pain.

"Can I have your attention? Everyone, please can I have your attention." Molly and I share the news. "Don't give up hope. We will have full equality. Don't give up hope." Easier said than done. The tears come quickly to everyone. I remember what it was like when the California State Supreme Court invalidated our marriage license in 2004, like getting the wind kicked out of you.

But it's not time for me to cry or show weakness. I have to be strong. I have to comfort my friends whose hopes have been dashed on the rocks.

Progressive clergy are among us and they offer to do blessings near the Harvey Milk bust in the rotunda for all couples who want their relationships blessed.

And then it's time to leave. Empty-handed couples without the marriage licenses they came for.

Mayor Gavin Newsom and County Assessor Recorder Phil Ting promising that they will be ready and waiting to marry people the second it's legal.

But will these couples get a chance next week? Or, are nuptials for same-sex couples in California still many months or even years away?

We will never give up hope!

You can take our fearless leader Harvey Milk, you can take away our marriage licenses, you can take away our constitutional right to marry, and you can delay justice and our wedding days; but we are love warriors and we will continue to love and fight for equality and justice for all! ∞

A Day in the Life of a Love Warrior

DAVINA
KOTULSKI, PH.D.

It's OK. I Love You.

— DAVINA KOTULSKI, PH.D.

During the California State Supreme Court Case challenge to Prop 8 in March 2009, I stood on the steps of the State Supreme Courthouse and was yelled at by Yes on 8 people holding anti-gay signs. One woman was literally screaming in my face and pointing her finger at me. You can see the back of my head here in the photo on this page.

Her adult daughter was with her. You can see they are holding a sign of a gay couple kissing with a red circle and a slash through it.

Usually, my hands would have trembled with rage in the face of people calling me names and screaming anti-gay epithets, but something powerful took hold of my heart and I was filled with compassion. Yep, compassion. The kind of compassion that Gandhi writes about. I truly felt love for my "enemies." I felt myself sending them love. And I began to mouth the words "It's okay. I love you." The young woman had to close her eyes. She could not meet my eyes that were committed to respecting her dignity and worth and refused to respond to her with anything less than love. I could feel her pain, or as we psychologists say, her cognitive dissonance.

I had a shocking personal breakthrough feeling energized with the spirit of love, smiling and singing "What the world needs now is love sweet love, it's the only thing that there's just too little of." We sang that line over and over and over again for at least 30 minutes. It was a healing shield from what was being hurled at us and kept my heart connected to why I was there because of love. Because I know my ability to love is equal to a heterosexual person's ability to love and that my love for another woman should be honored and cherished and respected the way the love between a man and a woman is.

90

I grasped the other marriage equality supporters and we held on to each other's shoulders and stood strong being the truth of who we are – lights of love, equality, justice and joy! You can't take that away from us, only we can put out that light. We will continue to emerge as love warriors dedicated to love and equality for all. And because we are a movement of love and equality, seeking liberty, justice, dignity, and respect for all, we must embody those qualities in all of our interactions with those who fear marriage equality and cannot yet see that the world becomes a better place when the bonds of unjust tradition are broken. Society's emotional IQ, our emotional quotient, rises when all are equal and discrimination is eradicated, and freedom from tyranny means a stronger, happier and healthier society for all.

It's Ok.
I Love You.

DAVINA
KOTULSKI, PH.D

As we move forward, claiming our equality, we must not become the bullies. We must not stoop to name calling or property damage or violence. We must hold ourselves in grace and dignity, with compassion for their choices knowing that many of them will one day awaken to their mistakes. Some will even apologize and may even become our allies as so many already have. ∞

91

Jolly Ranchers and Puzzle Pieces

— KITTY & CHERYLE LAMBERT-RUDD

ht

ees at the infa-
Grisanti brunch.
were only two
es that were taken
ay. Both were at
nators insistence.
ow l–r: Cheryle
Reverend Mother
Brauza (tan jacket
Ilar), Rita Sanchez,
ce Pacheco, Loui-
cher, Mary Hewitt,
ambert. Back row
van Ball, Jennifer
stino, Bruce Kogan
d behind Jen),
blyman Sam
Reverend Gerard
ns, Doug Charles
ly between Gerard
pug), Errin Doyle,
Bragg, Senator
Grisanti, Andrew
ardt.

ty Lambert-Rudd
hief of Staff, Doug
a.

ief of Staff, Doug
a, OUTspoken For
ty President, Kitty
ert-Rudd, Stone-
emocrat President,
Ball, and the
us Rita Sanchez.

There are so many amazing stories from the work that we did to get marriage passed in New York – but this one belongs to Western New York and the strong and dedicated activists of OUTspoken For Equality and Marriage Equality New York in the Buffalo, Niagara and Jamestown Region.

It all started when we lost a "yes vote" for marriage in the New York Senate in 2010 when Democrat, Antoine Thompson, lost to DOMA-supporting Republican, Mark Grisanti.

While discussing the problem at a small dinner party at our home one evening, one of our guests, Rita Sanchez, said she had an idea and wondered what we thought. The idea was to buy 1,324 of something and put it in a box – like a wedding gift – and give it to the new Senator, explaining just how many legal protections were not available to same-sex couples.

She had given it some thought and decided that the best representation would be an individually wrapped Jolly Rancher Candy for each of these rights. She would then wrap it up to look like a big wedding gift and present it to the Senator at our next visit to his office in Albany, NY, which was scheduled just weeks away in February (2011) with the mighty Marriage Equality New York (MENY).

Rita went above and beyond by wrapping each little candy with a paper that said "this represents just **one** of the 1,324 rights denied LGBT people."

We arrived in Albany with box in hand.

Anxiously, we waited for our appointment. We were emotionally set for NOT seeing the Senator, but just his staff. But we were not prepared for what happened when we met with his Chief of Staff, Doug Curella.

Rita brought the box to the table and explained to Mr. Curella that this

box represented the gift of marriage that every heterosexual couple gets by buying a $40 marriage license. That it represented the 1,324 New York State laws, responsibilities, and protections that were denied LGBT families.

She told him that the Senator had these. They were his. He could keep them all to himself, or give them away. He could share them, throw them out with the garbage, or he could put them in a closet and forget that he even had them.

She then took out a clear bag that she had placed 10 percent of the candies into. She explained that it was estimated that "just 10 percent of the population identifies as LGBT but, (she opened the bag and sprinkled the candies over the rest in the box) when you mix us into the population you can't really see us or our families, but we are there."

Mr. Curella looked at the big banker box sitting in front of him and bobbed his head up and down, politely.

It needs to be said that Ms. Sanchez is rather shy ... well, that is when she is Ms. Sanchez. When she is in her Drag King persona as Randy Strokes, he is a fireball! But she quietly sat down and looked at me. We both looked at him.

He said, "Well, thank you".

Damn! He doesn't get it ... he doesn't see the numbers!!! So, I stood up.

"May I pour these out on the desk and show you something? I promise to clean them all up and put them all back in the box." I asked.

He said, "Uh, sure."

I carefully dumped them in a very tight pile, mounded as tight and high as I could.

"If I may." (I began pushing down on the top of the pile, pushing them further and further out so that they became one single layer across the table top.) When they were spread all over the table, I picked up just one.

"Each of these represent a single New York State Law. A law that each person in this room (the room was **packed**) is denied access to."

In quick succession, I held up a single candy and said, "This one means the hospital doesn't have to tell me what the status of my life mate is. Even though we have five children together, they will make me ask our daughter, who lives in Arizona, about the status of my beloved. That actually happened to us. That family, who have been strangers for decades, can bar us from the bedside of a dying mate, simply because they don't approve of who/what we are.

This one means that one of us can't go get our kids out of school in an emergency or if they are sick, because we are a legal stranger to the child we helped birth, the **only** "other-parent" they have ever known.

This one means that even though we have paid for all the bills together for 10, 30, even 60+ years, that we have slept next to each other all those same years, built everything we have together, we will be left with nothing when the other dies. Even with a will, which can be contested and bankrupt us while simply fighting to keep our home, we will be forced to sell that home to pay a distant relative an inheritance they will take from the surviving partner or just to pay inheritance taxes.

This one means Bob can't inherit John's lobster and crab traps. Yeah, funny, unless Bob is dependent on making his living from the lobster traps in the business they built together.

This one means we have to pay **twice** for an adoption of one child, while it also means that you and your spouse only have to pay once to adopt that same child.

This one means that as employees that pay into our retirement funds at work, which is a requirement of our company, we have to live to collect it or no one gets it. If we die, our partners that are not spouses cannot collect our pensions.

And this one represents the same problem with our Social Security.

And this one represents that fact that when our partner dies and we own a home together, because we are not legally married, if only one of us is on the mortgage and it is **not** the survivor, the mortgage company can, and usually does, require a new mortgage or payment of the balance within 60 days putting us, once again, out of our homes.

This one says we can't access our own money. This one say we can't qualify for filing our taxes as married. This one says, in a heartbeat, the children we raised for the last 12 years are not ours. This one says we are not people … we are not families.

But all of these say we are voters. **All** of these are votes in the senator's district back home. As Rita pointed out (I scooped off about a hundred of the candies into a pile), this is the gay voters in that region. (I picked one up) This represents me. (I reached forward and picked up another from the small pile) this is my partner Cheryle. That is just two votes, right?"

He nodded.

"Wrong." (I reached into the big pile and started a pile in front of Mr. Curella.) "**This** one represents my daughter, this one my son-in-law. They are here today and sitting right there. They are straight. They love us. They support us. They vote. And this one represents Cher's boss, and these 20 are her coworkers. This one represents my neighbor across the street, and this one the neighbor next door …" This continued as I garnered a substantial pile in front of him.

"Each of these people, each of these voters, has sent you a letter in support of marriage equality. Please, **please** explain this to the Senator. Now is the time to do what is right. This state has always been a leader. The Senator has the opportunity to be one too. I am an eleventh-generation American citizen. How much longer do I, do **we**, need to beg for equal access to equal representation under existing law?"

Mr. Curella's posture had totally changed. He leaned forward and said, "This is something the Senator really **needs** to see."

Not being one to wait for another opportunity I said, "When can we meet with him? You name it, we will be there."

"Let's do it in district when the Senator is back home in Buffalo. Call me on Friday and we will set it up," he said.

Damn serious skippy! I was on that phone Friday and we set an appointment for the infamous Grisanti Brunch at El Museo Gallery for April! Senator Mark Grisanti, a Republican representing the 60th District in Western New York which ran all the way from Niagara Falls to the south end of Erie County, had agreed to an in-district sit-down with OUTspoken.

We all literally **floated** above the floor to the hallway where we could barely contain our unbridled joy! We had been told that we would **never** get an audience with the Senator. That we must go through another organization just to get a lobby appointment with him. That he was an absolute "NO vote" and that he was beholden to the Conservative Party. We didn't leave there with a yes vote but we left there with a foot in the door ... we left there with hope.

We all knew that an enormous amount of both research and planning had to go into this and it all had to be kept absolutely secret. This was going to be our first, and probably only, chance to educate the Senator on these issues. Our goal was to educate the Senator, not to bully him.

We researched his education, his career, his law firm, his family, his religious beliefs, his hobbies, his cultural background. We talked to people who knew him and got their insights. We talked to someone who knew, first hand, what could make a successful sit-down and what could make for a disastrous meeting.

We meticulously planned every, **every**, detail.

First and foremost it had to be a dark event. That sounds very covert, but we knew from our research that he was being targeted and bullied from the 'other side,' so we wanted to make it clear that we wanted to give him **facts** without **pressure**. We wanted to provide him **true and valid** information so that he could make an intelligent, logical and compassionate decision with his vote. There would be **no media**, no press release, no recordings, no pictures. **And no aggression**.

THE SETTING: We rented a local art gallery, El Museo Francisco Oller y Diego Rivera Art Gallery in Buffalo's "Gay Corridor." The food was important, and not just because we heard his wife, Maria, was an amazing cook. Nothing that must be touched with your hands, no mess, and no big chunks to try to chew while trying to converse. An OUTspoken and MENY member stepped up and gave us carte blanche for a food budget so Kanaiah Koutz, (our eldest daughter and a truly gifted gourmet cook), and her assistant, McKynna Miklos, (our granddaughter) could made chicken tortellini salad, fresh fruit, mini croissants, and tiramisu cups for dessert. We recruited members of OUTspoken and MENY to serve the food. **But there were strict controls**. They must serve quickly and then be gone. (Bless them all, they all hovered, quiet as mice, in the back hall and stairwell eavesdropping on the progress and never made a peep!) Teresa Watson kept the crew running smoothly – Terry Purdue, Ethan Robinson, Andrew Randazzo, and Amanda Kelley – each one dressed in black pants, white shirts, and looking so very sharp.

THE PARTICIPANTS: This was important. We made a list of every facet of the issue that affected us. Health care, education, credit, business ownership, inheritance, family dynamics, adoption, recognition of a second parent within the Family Court System or emergency/school situations, is Domestic Partnership or Civil Union the same as marriage and why not?, the role of religion, the constitutionality of recognizing one marriage but not another, senior aging without marriage protections in place, the right of legal redress through (God forbid) death or divorce. The complex way that all these questions and issues tie together for LGBT individuals but not for heterosexuals who purchase a $40 dollar piece of paper and instantly have 1,324 guaranteed New York State legislated protections that are then coupled with the 1000 plus protections awarded them under the Federal statutes governing marriage.

We chose very carefully who would sit at the table representing our community: Cheryle Rudd, Reverend Mother Ellen Brauza, Rita Sanchez, Candace Pacheco, Louisa Fletcher, Mary Hewitt, Kitty Lambert, Bryan Ball, Jennifer Diagostino, Bruce Kogan, Assemblyman Sam Hoyt, Reverend Gerard Williams, Doug Charles, Errin Doyle, James Bragg, and Andrew Eisenhardt.

THE PARTING GIFT ... A SIMPLE REMINDER: We knew that the Jolly Ranchers had had a profound impact. We wanted to keep that momentum and reinforce it to the Senator as he left. Once again, the brilliance of Rita Sanchez came through when she ordered a custom 1,000 piece puzzle of a picture of the Senator and his wife Maria and their son and daughter that was taken when they attended the Italian Festival here in Buffalo earlier that year. She counted out 100 random pieces (again, they represented that 10 percent of the population that identifies as LGBT) and put them in a mason jar. She then put the rest of the puzzle together and had it framed.

AND WE SAT DOWN: We started a bit late. (We all giggled that the Senator might have been standing us up or he was outside, watching, to see if press did show up. Things had been getting heated everywhere with press and pressure groups assaulting him from every side.) But when he arrived he was served a wonderful meal immediately and listened intently to our presentation. Rita

Sanchez gave him the gift of the framed puzzle of his family and explained that he would notice that there were about 10 percent of the pieces missing. She showed him the jar with 100 pieces in it.

"This picture represents your family, but is represents ours, too. We are the missing pieces, the ones that can't be a part of the current laws. Everyone has a family member that is gay or lesbian, possibly even transgender, even if they don't know it. We just want to be included equally in the protections we are promised by or state and federal constitution. When that happens, Senator, I promise to give you the 100 missing pieces of the puzzle." He was very moved by this. He stood up and hugged her and thanked us all.

We moved issue by issue, person by person around the table, the Senator asked great questions, really great questions, and was willing to look at it from a **legal** standpoint and not a **religious** one, though that remained a stumbling block for him. We had concluded our presentation and loaded him up with reading material. (Our research has told us he was a reader and a researcher.) For a brief moment, it was quiet, all eyes on him.

"I feel you deserve protections, there are no doubts about that, but I am just having trouble with the word. Marriage. I think that you would have less problem getting this passed if we could just find another word for it," he said thoughtfully. I must admit that I felt like screaming, and knew that everyone else at the table was struggling to control the same urge. I spoke first, something I often have no choice over. But this time I felt that I needed to put it in historical terms, in legal terms, in terms an attorney would understand.

"Senator, I get it. You know we need these protections." He nodded his head. "We each thirst after these protections and the rights and privileges that would protect our families." Again, he nodded his head. "Let's look at it as a well filled with protections, like water. You agree that everyone should get to drink from the well but when the water is run through the pipes, it should come out to your family at a fountain marked 'Marriage' and to my family as one marked 'For Gays Only.'"

He looked shocked, and then humbled and a bit sad. "Would that work for any other group in this country, Senator?" He seemed deep in thought.

"We are not willing, we will **not** settle for anything less than what our own siblings have. Full marriage equality. Because our families deserve equal access to equal protections under existing law. Nothing more. But certainly, nothing less."

Silence hung in the air. He made eye contact. My darling sitting next to me squeezed my hand so tight. We knew. He got it. Now we just had to pray he was strong enough to vote **Yes**.

The Senator didn't disappoint us. In fact, in his speech on the Senate floor he referred to the meeting and stated, "A man can be wiser today than yesterday, but there will be no respect for that man if he has failed in his duty to do the work. I cannot legally come up with an argument against same-sex marriage … I vote in the affirmative Mr. Secretary." ∞

Partners: Out4Immigration and Marriage Equality USA

— AMOS LIM

Mickey and I met/corresponded on April 21, 1995 online on a usenet message board about gay life. I was living in Singapore then, figuring out who I was and trying to find more information. He was just moving from Los Angeles to Bakersfield. I saw his posting about LGBT role models and long-term relationships and requested that he help me buy a book called, "Straight from the Heart" — a biography by Bob Paris and Rod Jackson. We started emailing each other and proceeded to speak over the phone almost daily, even though we are thousands of miles and many time zones apart.

When we finally met a year-and-a-half later in Singapore, we realized that we had already fallen in love with each other. We continued the long distance relationship while trying to find a way for me to come to the United States. As our relationship was not recognized by the federal government due to DOMA, there was no way for him to sponsor me for a fiancé visa. At the same time, an H1-B Visa, to enable me to work in the United States, was expensive and very difficult to obtain. After about two years of trying without success, we made the decision that I should apply to a college here to get my MBA with a student visa, and hopefully, would be able to find gainful employment that would lead to a green card.

In the meantime, Mickey moved to San Francisco in 1997, deciding that Bakersfield was too conservative for him. He found a binational couple support group called Lesbian and Gay Immigration Task Force (LGIRTF) in San Francisco that met monthly at the office of National Center for Lesbian Rights (NCLR) and joined them. When I finally was granted a student visa and accepted at a college in San Rafael, I packed my bag, said goodbye to my family in Singapore, and moved here. That was the start of our activism advocating for equal immigration rights for same-sex couples. In 2006, a small group of activist binational couples decided to step up our game and founded a grassroots organization called Out4Immigration, for the purposes of educating the public about our issues and empowering same-sex binational couples to tell their stories and speak out.

Marriage Equality USA was one of the first groups to support same-sex binational couples when a group of us started advocating for equal immigration rights for same-sex couples. They provided us a platform to speak during their rallies, so that we could educate the public about the issues facing binational couples, something that both the immigrant community and the LGBT community had resisted. Those communities feared that our issue would muddle the fights for immigration rights and marriage equality, but MEUSA welcomed us with open arms; in fact, they oftentimes reached out to us. When we decided to branch out and start Out4Immigration, they were very supportive and continued to help us get our message out!

I should also add, at this point NCLR was the other national prominent LGBT group that supported and stood with us all the way from the beginning, providing us with fiscal support and a meeting place as LGIRTF, and continuing to support us when we started Out4Immigration.

I personally believe MEUSA's support brought a greater awareness about our issue to the public officials who spoke at the rallies, and to anybody who attended the rallies. I noticed politicians incorporating same-sex immigration rights as a talking point when addressing the 1,138 rights that married couples have that domestic partnerships and civil unions do not provide.

I am, and will forever be, thankful for the open hands of support that MEUSA provided us, for MEUSA walking the journey with us, for understanding the issue without much explaining, for just saying, "Of course, you should speak on stage … come on!" instead of giving us excuses. I know that I will forget some names but a huge thank you to Molly McKay, Davina Kotulski, John Lewis, Stuart Gaffney, Billy Bradford, Christine Allen, Dennis Veite, and many, many others for their support, for their help, and for being our friends on this incredible civil rights journey fighting for marriage equality and immigration equality! ∞

Standing up by Sitting In

— ZACK LYONS

"I can't believe they are doing this today. Don't they understand what they are doing to our special day?" I overhear this comment from an angry woman waiting for her turn at the Clerk's Office in San Francisco City Hall. It is Valentine's Day, and in contrast to her dark mood, she is dressed in a beautiful white wedding gown. One of the other people with our group also overhears her and says simply, "At least you'll still get your license today. We're here because we can't get one." I have only a few moments to watch her scowling reaction before we continue our walk down the long marble hallway into the Clerk's Office. I feel a myriad of emotions all at once. Anger at her irritation, nervousness about what I'm doing (who am I?), and elation to finally be doing something concrete for the movement.

I can't say exactly what brought me to decide to participate in my first act of civil disobedience. I joked off-the-cuff that I turned 33, my Jesus birthday, and it was time to do something Christ-like with my time. I just knew it was time for me to take a stand. And, while that was a thrilling and exciting decision at first, now that I'm sitting on the Clerk's Office floor, surrounded by police, media, and my fellow Love Warriors, I can hardly think over the deafening pounding coming from my chest. I am as nervous as I can remember ever being, but thankfully, the calming Love Warriors are seated in a circle on the dark green carpet. The ring includes some old friends like Billy Bradford and Kip Williams and some new (but lasting) friends like Rev. Karen Oliveto and Rev. Roland Stringfellow.

We are quietly singing along to We Shall Not Be Moved, when the officer with the bullhorn interrupts us with a blaring, "This is your final warning.

102

If you fail to disburse, you will be arrested." A handful of people on the edge of our circle shuffle out of the Clerk's Office, and I realize that I'm gripping the hands of the Love Warriors next to me a little too tightly. I take a few deep breaths and finally relax. It's too late now and instead of being stressed, I feel empowered. I draw strength from the people in the room with me, the unknown individuals across the country who deserve full recognition by their government, and the office upstairs where then-Supervisor Harvey Milk was assassinated. The police are reluctant to process us, but they begin to cuff us with zip ties, one by one, and escort us out of the room. All the while, Love Warriors are championing their cry. I am ... Somebody ... And I deserve ... Full Equality ... Right Here, Right Now.

An hour later and our circle of Love Warriors are in a dark holding cell somewhere in the bowels of City Hall. We're standing now, but our hands are still bound behind us with zip tie handcuffs. Despite the venue, we are smiling and giddy, cracking an odd joke as we wait to be processed. Kip stands in front of everyone and tells them that I asked to be a part of the action as my 33rd birthday present. Without pause, every Love Warrior sings Happy Birthday to me in that holding cell. To date, it is the best rendition of that song that I have ever heard!

When I look back on the arc of my experiences in the marriage equality movement, this one shines brightly for me. I can recall the smell and sounds of the day, even though the day itself went by in a hasty haze. The clacking of our shoes on the marble floors throughout City Hall, the musty smell in the basement holding cell, the feeling of being hit simultaneously with sunshine and cheers as we finally left the building, it's all still crystalline for me. The truth is, I think this is the day that I fully committed myself to the cause, and I went far outside of my comfort zone in the process. I reflect on that upset bride-to-be who may have become an ally. I reflect on the spirit and strength of the community who nurtured my individual growth and the growth of the movement. I am a better citizen, friend, and everyday activist because of their involvement. Because of my experiences with marriage equality, I strive to be a better ally and push forward into other frontiers: #BlackLivesMatters, trans* equality, and access to basic healthcare and education in impoverished countries. ∞

Standing up
by Sitting In

ZACK LYONS

A Movement Begins

— CATHY MARINO-THOMAS

My wife, Sheila, always wanted a wedding, white picket fence, family, etc. She dreamed about it and talked about this dream often. I, being a loving partner, wanted to try to make that dream come true.

In 1995, we had a wedding. We had friends, accepting family, a service in a Unitarian Church in Stamford, CT, a reception. No marriage license. We felt married. We honored each other as if we were legally married. But, alas, the world did not.

Once we came down from the euphoria and realized absolutely nothing had changed, we knew we had to seek like-minded people and try to change the law of the land. We discovered Marriage Equality New York (MENY). We found out, through the LGBT Center of NYC, that they were a small group of eight people working toward change. We were excited to meet them and so began our 20+ year relationship with the group.

Our very first action was the Brooklyn Pride Parade. Five of us marched, two signs each — not many paid attention and those that did thought we were crazy. It went on like that for a while.

After I had given birth to our daughter in 2000 and returned to work with the group, President Bush decided he was going to put forward an amendment to the Constitution that would bar any chance marriage equality would ever come to the USA. Bronx State Senator Ruben Diaz Sr. loved this idea and decided he would put together a rally in support. We had to respond, so we begged around 25 activists to come with us to the Bronx in support of our protest. We thought we had such a huge number of people and, on the way to the Bronx location, we were feeling pretty strong. We had our people, our signs,

105

and our determination.

Our determined group stepped out of the subway, into a sea of 5,000 people in support of Senator Diaz's rally. The streets were completely full with Evangelist Bible Thumpers shouting their support of our permanent discrimination. Thankfully, the NYPD came to our rescue – we were being penned in for our own protection. We shouted back at the opposition – we tried to be as loud as possible, but we were afraid – very afraid. That day, we stuck it out – we protested and did get some publicity for our efforts. We had to be escorted out of the area by the NYPD in a heart-thumping escape from the hate!

We left feeling energized by our action. We now knew what the opposition looked like and how hateful they were. But, nothing was going to stop us. We were determined. A movement had begun. ∞

The First MENY Wedding March

− CATHY MARINO-THOMAS

Our marriage movement was picking up steam. There were more and more people interested in the idea of equal marriage. We were convincing people. We were teaching about the over 1,300+ things that can only be gained with a legal marriage license, and people were listening. But it wasn't enough. We still did not really have the ear of many legislators and we knew that's what we needed.

Around 2004, MENY held a strategy session at the LGBT Center. The Center gave us a space and then had to give us even more as the activists came in droves for the discussion. Lots of ideas were thrown around that night. Someone proposed a march across the Brooklyn Bridge', which was appealing to all, and the planning began.

We would march across the bridge − close it down if possible − from Manhattan to Brooklyn. We would carry umbrellas in the colors of our rainbow flag. We would schedule speakers in Cadman Plaza park at the end. We would invite press and talk to them about how our families suffered without the legal right to marry. We would begin what was a winning strategy − telling our stories. We would make people understand, even if they knew no gay people, how important "I Do" and a legal license was.

We were very nervous the morning of the march. We did, in fact, get a couple of equality minded legislators to come and speak, but, not many. The first to sign on was Congressman Jerry Nadler − a tireless supporter. But, we were concerned that no one would come to march. Thankfully, we were wrong! Over 1,000 people attended that very first march and it was an astounding success. It became an annual event for the next five years and morphed into a fundraiser for our movement. When we first took over the Brooklyn Bridge, only the Gay

City News and the NY Daily News covered the event. By the time we held the fifth march, the media was clamoring to tell our story and politicians were begging to speak. It was fabulous and quite a spectacle. Our beautiful rainbow! We added t-shirts and the sight was stunning. ∞

—

CATHY
ARINO–THOMAS

1   Bridge Walks (aka The Wedding March) were begun in 2004 by MENY in New York City and eventually spreading to locations across the state and to San Francisco, community members marched to symbolize crossing the "bridge" to equality. Midway during the walk, organizers traditionally held a long-distance call between marchers crossing the Brooklyn Bridge and those crossing the Golden Gate Bridge.

I Love to Cry at Weddings

— MICHAEL MARKIEWICZ

I have never referred to myself as an activist, but rather as someone who cares deeply for issues in which I get involved. I remember the day when Governor Cuomo signed the marriage equality bill into law in New York State. It was just before the Gay Pride parade in New York in 2011. I remember giving him a big shout out as he marched past me that day. The big smile on his face (not specifically directed at me, but rather at the entire crowd) filled me with a sense of honor and awe. Finally, we had a major politician who recognized us as first-class citizens. I never thought I would experience that feeling again anytime soon.

Prior to, and after that momentous day, in my work as a CPA and Certified Financial Planner, I often lectured on financial, estate and tax planning for same-sex couples. Included in that discussion was the question of whether couples should wed at all, given the significant potential financial and tax implications included in that. I always prefaced that discussion by saying that the decision has an emotional aspect to it, which I would not speak about in my capacity as a CPA and Certified Financial Planner. That was something that would have to be left to the couples themselves.

In 2011 I was approached by the executive director of Marriage Equality USA, Brian Silva, and he asked me to serve as finance director of Marriage Equality USA. Brian connected with me through our mutual membership in the National Gay and Lesbian Chamber of Commerce New York City. I was honored to be asked to serve in this role.

Fast forward to 2014. Just one week prior to the SCOTUS decision, I was asked to be on a panel at a major financial institution to discuss the "what if's" should

left–right

Mark Miller and Michael Markiewi[cz]

Wedding Day.

109

SCOTUS rule to make same-sex marriage legal across the land. I recall being asked by a member of the audience whether I thought SCOTUS would rule in our favor. I couldn't answer the question, although I did say that I was hopeful. One week later, the sense of pride and jubilation was like something I had rarely experienced in my life. My life partner and I went to the rally in the West Village, and the sea of rainbow flags and banners filled me with pride and joy.

In November of 2014, my then partner and I decided to wed. We married at City Hall the day before Thanksgiving. Even though this was a small ceremony, it was momentous for us, as we finally had the legal right to do what every straight couple had the right to do. We both beamed with joy and elation. New York courts have a procedure by which a couple applies for a marriage license, waits two days, and then returns for the actual marriage to take place. We asked the judge for a judicial waiver, waited two hours (not days) and we were wed. The overwhelming emotion that overcame me realizing that we were now equal under the law, and that our marriage was legally recognized filled me with a sense of emotional pride. I also felt like a giddy school kid.

Both sadly and happily, I am seeing my role at Marriage Equality USA coming to a close as the organization is closing its doors, having fulfilled this incredible mission of the freedom to marry for all Americans. Nothing has made me prouder than to be a part of this amazing organization, particularly as marriage equality became the law of the land during my tenure. I'm grateful to everyone at Marriage Equality USA and other activists in the numerous other equality organizations throughout the country for making it all a reality. There is yet much work to do, but I am proud to have been a small part of it. ∞

8 the Play Brings the Prop 8 Story to Off-Broadway

— BRIAN MASCHKA

When I became the Artistic Director for the 2012 Fresh Fruit Festival, I began preparing to present the best theater, music, comedy, dance, and film made by and for LGBTQ audiences. It seemed to be the perfect forum and audience to present a staged reading of *8* the play by Academy Award-winning screenwriter Dustin Lance Black. The play utilizes the original transcripts and is an unprecedented account of the 2010 Perry v. Schwarzenegger (now Perry v. Brown) case, which sought to overturn the 2008 voter-approved Prop. 8 legislation that denied same-sex couples the right to marry. The trial ultimately led to a California federal judge's ruling that Prop. 8 was unconstitutional and unfairly discriminated against homosexuals. The play was presented under license from the American Foundation for Equal Rights at The Wild Project in the East Village on July 27, 2012 to a sold-out audience.

I assembled a fantastic cast of theater luminaries, both Broadway and Off-Broadway.

The cast featured Stephen Mo Hanan (Chief Judge Vaughn R. Walker), Roger Rees (Charles J. Cooper), and Rick Elice (David Blankenhorn). They were joined by Stacia Newcomb (clerk), Ben Franklin (broadcast journalist), Michael Mastro (Theodore B. Olson), Patrick Husted (David Boies), Bryan Jarrett (Jeff Zarrillo), Sam Rosen (Paul Katami), Randy Graff (Sandy Stier), Karen Oster (Kris Perry), Scott Pearson (Elliott), Mark Fisher (Spencer), Rachel Burttram (Dr. Nancy Cott), Susan Louise O'Connor (Maggie Gallagher), Sanjiv Jhaveri (Dr. Ilan Meyer), David Turner (Ryan Kendall), Brendan Powers (Dr. Gregory Herek), Destan Owens (Dr. Gary Segura), Peter Kim (Dr. William Tam), and Al Sapienza (Evan Wolfson).

top–bottom

Reading of *8* at the Fruit Festival. (201

l–r: Brian Maschka Cathy Marino-Tho Fred Anguera and MEUSA Executive Director Brian Silv ticipate in an audi talkback following reading of *8* at the Fruit Festival. (201

Reading of *8* at the Fruit Festival. (201

111

Following the staged reading, I led a lively discussion with leaders from Marriage Equality New York: Brian Silva, Fred Anguera and Cathy Marino-Thomas.

I'm so happy that we were able to tell the story of Prop 8 and to make our support known for true marriage equality for all Americans. ∞

Real Housewives of New York on the March

— ALEX MCCORD & SIMON VANKEMPEN

Alex's recollection ...

It was 2010 at the end of a sweaty summer, and we were gearing up to start production of the fourth season of the *Real Housewives of New York City*. Simon and I had previously been in contact with Marriage Equality New York, and they reached out to us to participate in the 7th annual Wedding March, a peaceful march of activism across the Brooklyn Bridge. We were delighted to get involved, and pitched the march as a potential segment to the *RHoNY* producers, got the green light and began planning. I suggested that the cast wear wedding gowns for dual reasons; first, to make an activist statement; drivers across the Brooklyn Bridge are used to seeing marches and often don't know what they are for. I thought that if the public passing by saw lots of wedding gowns, it might help raise visual awareness for MENY. Second, from a production standpoint, having the cast in wedding gowns would make for splashy TV, and give the opportunity for getting ready scenes and after party scenes, any of which could lead to the type of drama that drives the show and cement the likelihood that the footage would make the final edit. Should I insert a "be careful what you wish for here?" Oy.

Anytime an event is being filmed for a reality show, there are loads of emails, texts and calls back and forth between production and talent, and the final approach to filming always morphs. We learned that we'd have LuAnn, Sonja and Kelly marching, and that Sonja had been approached by MENY to join the twenty-or-so speakers on the roster, as we had. We combed the city's costume rental places to find a rainbow tuxedo jacket for Simon, and I got my wedding gown and veil out of storage and ready to go. We decided with MENY's bless-

113

ing that Simon would speak instead of me; he wanted to make the point that without marriage equality, immigration law made it impossible for multi-national couples to remain together in the States legally. This was just one reason behind our support of marriage equality; it's a basic human right that should be available to everyone. Since we knew speeches needed to be two to three minutes tops, we chose immigration as the focus.

The morning of the march, a getting-ready scene was set to film at Sonja's house. When I arrived, I immediately noticed Sonja being strangely aggressive, cutting me off mid-sentence and reminding me it was "her day." I had no idea what she was talking about, and finally asked a producer, who explained that Sonja was now the grand marshal of the parade. "Fantastic, she'll eat that up," was more or less my thought at the time. The conversation between the girls did seem like it was going far, far away from marriage equality, and I kept trying to bring it back, annoying the rest of the cast. Still, that was a fairly normal occurrence – by season four I had to bark and bite at the ladies in order to get their attention, so that was business as usual.

A couple of hours later, we arrived at Foley Square in front of the Supreme Court building. As we assembled in a VIP area behind the stage with all the participants such as the host, Appollonia Cruz and Senator Tom Duane, Simon and I were told that we'd been removed from the speaking roster per Sonja's request. We both saw red, but not for the reasons the cast or others thought. Almost immediately, we realized that the producers played each one of us; they had orchestrated the last minute grand marshal addition, the removal of our speech and were trying their level best to stir up trouble. Sonja, bless her, was not one to see through those off-camera manipulations, a quality that led to her being the perfect mark for producers to lead into temptation. In fact, the day was about marriage equality, not heteros arguing. After a few minutes of surreptitious squabbling, we realized in horror that we had become the ones pulling focus, not Sonja, and we should not say one. more. word. We stepped back and let events unfold. Sonja gave her speech, the crowd marched through the rain with rainbow colored umbrellas and the voices in my head were keeping me sane by whispering that even though Simon and I were going to look

114

like jerks, marriage equality was hopefully going to get some good screen time because of all the drama.

After the march, we filmed an after-party scene at our townhouse in Cobble Hill, where Simon made his immigration speech. We also had some remarks from a dear friend from college, and I thought it was particularly appropriate that the filmed segment ended with remarks from a married gay man.

Fast-forward to late 2016, and Simon and I are now living in his native Australia, where it's a bit disconcerting that marriage equality is not yet the law. I hope that soon, parliament here will follow the lead of SCOTUS and make it so.

And Simon says ...

I have just re-watched that *RHoNY* episode again some six years after the MENY March and I am so glad to say almost everything in it has now been consigned to U.S. history. That Wedding March took place in September 2010, this episode aired April 2011 and just three months after that, in July 2011 New York State finally passed legislation allowing marriage for all which Governor Cuomo promptly signed into law. Of course, it took another five years until SCOTUS ruled in June 2015 in Obergefell v. Hodges for it to be recognized across all 50 states, something I trust will not change now that President Obama no longer holds the trump card for future appointments to SCOTUS.

The process of filming reality TV (something I am glad to say is now in my past) can be dramatic in and of itself, and after a while you get used to producer tricks which are predicated on the creation of conflict — a staple of *Real Housewives* and other reality shows.

Without this orchestrated conflict the Wedding March segment on *RHoNY* may have been reduced to 30 seconds of "B roll." Instead the 15 minutes or so of TV time that it became created awareness about marriage for all via osmosis with *RHoNY*'s viewers.

Remember that this aired over five years before Oberfegell and at that time swaths of middle America (*RHoNY*'s core audience) were either against marriage equality, ignorant about it, or at the very least ambivalent about it.

115

This is not to overstate the effect of this *RHoNY* episode – just recognizing that it was one drop among millions that finally propelled SCOTUS to determine that social mores had sufficiently changed to where the 14th amendment could be used to eliminate inequality under U.S. marriage laws.

It now seems such a kerfuffle over who could speak and at what time but ultimately after the march I did get to have my say that day, albeit within the confines of Alex and my home surrounded by others from the show's cast. But more important, it was with two other same-sex couples who now benefit from the change of law and the fact that states since 2015 have had to recognize their relationship no differently than they would Alex's and mine. My speech which did air in that episode was meant to highlight how U.S. immigration laws discriminated against fellow U.S. citizens and it went as follows:

"Ah well, what I was going to say is that, 11 years ago I came to this country from my native Australia for what I thought would be three weeks. I met an Alex. (Kelly Bensimon interjects "an Alex"?) Well I met an Alex and fortunately the Alex that I met was Alexandra and not Alexander because if Alexandra had been Alexander then I couldn't have got a fiancé visa, I couldn't have got a Green Card and I couldn't have become a U.S. citizen."

Of course after that scene at home *RHoNY* editors had to cut to Sonja's talking head segment so she could question my sexuality and so on which was and is completely beside the point that I was trying to make ... but whatever. At the end of the day I am just so happy knowing that fiancé visas are now available for any non-US citizen who falls in love with a U.S. citizen irrespective of their gender and trust that recent turns in U.S. presidential politics won't reverse that incredible progress for equality for all anytime soon. ∞

116

Love in a Time of Exile

— MARTHA MCDEVITT-PUGH

On May 4, 2001, my wife and I became the first Australian-American[1] same-sex couple to marry, part of the first wave of same-sex marriages in the world. It was a moment that changed our lives forever, in ways we couldn't imagine.

Flashback to the end of 1998 when I fell in love with my best friend, Lin, who had lived in the Netherlands for the past two decades.

I was living in the San Francisco Bay Area, where I had a life of wonderful challenges, full to the brim. I was exactly where I wanted to be. Near my mother, siblings, and six nieces and nephews. I had a job I loved managing an award-winning team, with many wonderful colleagues and opportunities to grow and develop myself.

And then, a 16-year friendship turned to love. It knocked us both off our feet when we discovered a soulmate who had been there all along.

We spent what seemed like an eternity in a long distance relationship, phoning at night, before I went to sleep and just as she was waking up in the morning, emailing every day, meeting up for weekends in California, when Lin would hop over while on a business trip at the UN in New York. I'd make the trip to Europe when I could. Following the advice of a dear friend who'd made a bi-coastal California-Maine relationship work for an extended period, we made a point to see each other at least every six weeks.

Less than a year into our long-distance romance, Lin asked me to join her in the Netherlands. Her son was about to start his last year of high school and she felt it was not the right time to leave him. She was willing to join me in the USA, but not for another two years. I said yes — of course I would move to the Netherlands. My heart told me it was inevitable. We were meant to be together.

left–right

Madrid Pride. (200

Martha delivering
to Gov. Schwarzen
asking him not to v
the marriage bill i

Wedding Day.
Photo credit: Gon Bu

117

I said yes without hesitating, but also without fully grasping what it truly meant to leave behind a career in Silicon Valley, to miss seeing my nieces and nephews grow up, and to start a new life in a new country. I said yes because I also knew that for her to join me in the USA would require jumping through nearly impossible immigration hurdles whereas in the Netherlands, unmarried partners had been recognized for immigration purposes, regardless of gender, for decades. As a Dutch resident, all Lin had to do was declare that I was her partner.

And so we started our journey as a binational same-sex couple. There was much to learn. In the USA most immigration is defined by marriage or blood. I couldn't sponsor her as my family member. In the eyes of U.S. law, we were legal strangers, unable to marry, and there was nothing we could do about that. The Defense of Marriage Act (DOMA) stated unequivocally that no marriage between two women or two men could be federally recognized by the U.S. government. That meant that the federal agency responsible for issuing green cards for family members had never issued one to a same-sex partner.

That all started to change in the year we started our long distance romance. The Netherlands had come close to granting marriage rights to all citizens in 1998, changing the legislation to a watered-down "registered partnership" in the end. The Netherlands was hardly the first country in Europe to recognize same-sex relationships, as Denmark had done a decade earlier. Until 1998, Dutch couples, straight or gay, could access many of the rights of married couples by going to a lawyer and drawing up a not very romantic "cohabitation contract," but there was no legal way to register a same-sex relationship.

In 1999, just as I was preparing to move to the Netherlands, the compromise that brought about registered partnerships started to unravel. Through sharing stories about their lives and the impact of the lack of access to the same rights as heterosexual couples, LGBT couples began to generate support for full-blown marriage rights. After 20 years of persistent campaigning by activists, with support from a few politicians who stuck out their necks in support of something that had never been done anywhere in the world, a shift in public opinion led to key government officials' support for marriage rights for all.

It was an exciting time for Lin and me, as we followed the news of the proposed change to make marriage law gender neutral. When it became likely that the law would change, Lin asked me to marry her and I said yes. We told a few friends we planned to marry when the law changed. And then we got on with our lives.

That's how I landed in a country that was on the verge of being the first in the world to open up marriage to same-sex couples.

We became marriage equality activists in the weeks and months leading up to our wedding. We had no role models for how to marry as two women. Being excluded from marriage, we hadn't paid much attention to the details at any of the weddings we'd attended or been a part of. We had a learning curve.

We shopped for wedding accessories, only to thrill shopkeepers that we were buying not one, but two pairs of white shoes and handmade silk hats. The world was about to see the first same-sex nuptials. It was exciting and fun to share our plans with the florist at the end of our block, the Italian owner of the restaurant where we'd hold our wedding dinner, and the celebrant from the city of Amsterdam who would marry us. We experienced the love and support of our friends, family, neighbors and total strangers.

We realized that marrying as a binational couple in the first country in the world to have the courage to include same-sex couples gave us an opportunity to create a bridge to a new future, a world where all families are honored and respected.

Our wedding turned into a week-long celebration, with family and friends flying in from the USA, Australia, the UK and Germany. The Advocate magazine published my first-person story about what I saw as the future for the USA: marriage equality, where all couples would have the choice to have their family bond recognized through marriage. A future where signatures on a piece of paper and speaking the simple words "Yes, I do," would unite two people in front of friends and family, and create a commitment to live into, no matter what.

We realized that we had a unique opportunity to share what marriage equality looked like by sharing our story.

We learned that being open about who we are, hiding nothing, was empowering. The first time it unfolded at the airport immigration counter, the immigration officer got very official, turned his attention to Lin, and asked her the standard questions: how long are you staying in the USA, what is the purpose of your visit, and what is your relationship with each other? When she answered that she was visiting her in-laws and offered to show him our wedding album, he quickly said no thank you and stamped our passports. But we'd piqued his curiosity. As we started to leave to go to the baggage claim area, he asked, "Is that a … legal contract?" Having conversations to educate immigration officials became one of our pleasures in life.

As joyous as it was to be legally married, traveling home to the USA was always a reminder of how limited our rights still were. In 2002, we reached out to Marriage Equality California and Immigration Equality. Inspired to start a movement of LGBT U.S. citizens locked out of the USA because their relationships were not recognized, we organized an initiative to celebrate and unite the LGBT "exile" community. Nearly every Dutch person we spoke with knew an American who had left the USA to be with a same-sex partner. We chose Thanksgiving 2002 as the night to celebrate the Netherlands as the first country to open up marriage to couples of all genders. The first Love Exiles Thanksgiving dinner brought together dozens of Dutch-US LGBT couples and their children and drew media coverage telling the story of LGBT Americans excluded from their own country because of who they loved. Thus was the start of organizing our community over the next 11 years to tell their stories and create visibility for love exiles to build support for changing U.S. immigration law.

In 2004, I joined the Marriage Equality Express, traveling from Oakland, CA to Washington DC with 50 other marriage equality activists from California. We spoke at 14 cities along the way and met with small groups of LGBT Americans in state capitals across the country, telling the stories of the countless marriages invalidated in San Francisco's 2004 "Winter of Love" and families torn apart and lives shattered by DOMA. Throughout it all, we stood for the day we would be included in the fundamental human right to form a family.

The movement was starting to gain public support.

My hope of returning to the USA was dashed in November 2004, when George Bush was re-elected. With Bush in the White House, the Uniting American Families Act (UAFA), which would include LGBT couples in U.S. immigration law, stood no chance of becoming law.

Democrats Abroad embraced our cause, passing one of the first resolutions calling for LGBT couples to be recognized by U.S. immigration law. With its status as a state in the Democratic Party, Democrats Abroad sent LGBT delegates from the love exile community to the Democratic National Convention in 2004, 2008 and 2012, and lobbied members of congress to support UAFA.

I was elected as a delegate to the Democratic National convention in 2012, representing Democrats Abroad. Arriving in the convention hall the first evening, I reached under my seat to find the party platform, and was moved to tears to see our community mentioned: same-sex partners, with no access to green cards and no other avenues to keep their families together, would be low priority for deportation. While it was not yet the change that would bring America's love exiles home, it was a sign of the change that was on its way.

In the 11 years we ran the Love Exiles Foundation, we met extraordinary and inspiring people, LGBT and straight, who saw as we did, that love is love, and loving couples who make a commitment to share their lives deserve the same rights. We forged friendships, submitted testimony, and attended a congressional hearing, empowering our community to speak up and speak out in their communities and in the media.

We watched the number of places with marriage equality spread in Europe, Canada, Massachusetts and Connecticut, South Africa, Latin America, Mexico City and briefly in 2008, to my home state of California.

As more and more couples were able to marry, we saw the conversation for immigration equality shift. To those of us living in the new future of marriage equality and seeing support of our straight allies, friends and family grow steadily, a new pathway emerged to win the right to live in the USA. We'd lobbied for our families to be included in the long overdue immigration reform bill, and we had support from a number of senators and members of congress to add LGBT families to the proposed law. But with so many of us legally married, it remained a long shot to add new concepts like "permanent same-sex partners" to existing laws. All that was needed was to strike down the egregious law that stood in the way of recognition. DOMA had to go.

It took an octogenarian widow, Edie Windsor, to successfully challenge DOMA. The lives of American's exiles were changed forever on June 26, 2013, when DOMA's provisions that stood in the way of our immigration rights were struck down.

The marriage equality movement is one of the highlights of my life. I'll be forever grateful for the friends I made, the allies who supported us, and the ways our community came together to make change happen. It takes a village to make change and in the case of America's love exiles, the village was a global one. ∞

—

1   As far as we know, we were the first Australian-American same-sex married couple. An Australian male couple married just before we did, as did several American-Dutch couples.

Complaint Department and Organizational Recruiter

— MOLLY MCKAY

> *On April 10, 2016, Marriage Equality USA hosted one of several 20-year anniversary parties in San Francisco. As a long-time leader in the organization, Molly McKay was asked to share her thoughts on our work. These are her remarks.*

What a joy it is to reflect and celebrate these 20 golden years of Marriage Equality USA, this mighty grassroots organization that could — to stand together and mark this milestone of the official end of the long campaign, the journey to justice that ends with the words "Mission Accomplished!" Marriage Equality USA, Marriage Equality USA!

And yes, we have so many organizations and leaders to thank and include in this celebration, and yes, Marriage Equality USA has always been at the forefront of facilitating and involving everyone who wanted to join in on collaboration and coalition building, But tonight. Since it is just us. I wanted to take a minute to just focus and maybe even brag a little bit about our unique role in helping see this shared dream into reality.

We Marriage Equality USA folks have walked this long fabulous journey together with a servant's heart; We served and gave everything we had, without pay. Lord knows our organization was never the recipient of large grants or well-funded donors; most of what we raised came from shaking buckets on street corners and asking our friends, families and our own wallets to share what they could. But we had a shared vision, a shared dream, and an organization that housed a small yet extremely tenacious, talented and dedicated group of people who simply refused to accept anything less than full equality

left–right

Molly McKay spea
at one of the MEU
Year Anniversary
in San Francisco.
*Photo credit: Lawren
Gerald*

Uptown Dance for
Equality, Oakland
(2010)
Photo credit: Kirsten

123

for same-sex couples. Period.

When we started out, it seemed like we were reaching for the stars, with established LGBT organizations and even friendly elected officials telling us we were asking for too much, too soon (Senator Leno and Gavin Newsom being the notable exceptions), that organizing a bus trip for marriage equality across the country to D.C. would lose the Democrats the presidency, that showing up in wedding garb at marriage counters was silly and counterproductive because it made straight people uncomfortable. We were told to just sit back and let the paid staff do the behind-the-scene work to secure us a few relationship protections here and there – to sit down, be quiet, write checks, and not rock the boat.

Complaint
partment and
Organizational
Recruiter

MOLLY MCKAY

But we, the rebellious energizer bunnies of the movement, insisted on participating in our own liberation. We knew in our hearts that to secure our equality we had to get brave and step out into the light and, as Ellen Pontac says, flood the world with our truth to share our lives, our loves, our stories and to help find and encourage others to do the same. If you do a Google search for marriage equality and hit images, worldwide in newspapers we can't even translate, you will see photos of our grassroots folks, smiling, kissing, celebrating, and marrying – and that is what touched hearts, got the light bulbs to turn on; we were the stand, the picture that said a 1000 words, the example of courageous Americans standing up for liberty and justice for all. I've heard that other campaigns are trying to study our movement to determine what was the magic formula that made such dramatic social change in only 20 years.

With Marriage Equality USA's grassroots chapter leaders in each local community organizing events, and speaking to local media, catching the wave of media that came from all the court cases, and legislative hearings, and vetoes, and Prop 8 votes, we ensured that people understood the stakes weren't theoretical – it wasn't some amorphous gay community in the big cities that was affected – but rather, our friends, our neighbors, our co-workers, that nice lesbian couple that own the coffee shop down the street.

And Marriage Equality USA also reached into our own communities, with our various specific community liaisons to represent the diversity of our community and connect and share the commonalities of historical legal discrimination and shared cultural values which other mainstream organizations just didn't do. Maya and the Quilt project still travels the world making change and that was done with donated fabric and people who didn't know how to sew but wanted these stories told so we figured out how to do it. And we did this work never criticizing our opposition — we should thank them for being such perfect villains and counterparts to what we stood for — we did it with fun and creative lyrics to popular songs and Christmas carols and creativity.

Our organization served as a vehicle to manifest people's visions, ideas, projects, and offerings. We virtually never said "no;" we said "let's figure out how to use this donation or what we need and who might have what we need to make this event happen." We collected stories after Prop 8 passed and spoke truth to power about the hard truths that caused us to lose that oh so winnable battle so that we could employ that wisdom moving forward to learn, heal and eventually win the war nationwide.

And of course, one of my favorite duties was serving the dual role as complaint department and organizational recruiter. Woe to the unsuspecting who shared what the organization was missing and could do better, as the response was almost always the same: "You are absolutely right, you have identified a key issue we are not addressing and it seems YOU are the perfect person to change that — how would you like to serve as our new leader for that?" How many of you did I personally ask to step way out of your comfort zone to do something for the movement? I loved the look of panic when handing the microphone to an unsuspecting new leader and said "and now we will hear from our new leader on what they are doing that we should all get behind — speak!" And that is when magic happened, we all grew in this work, we became more than what we thought we could be and this work brought out the very best in all of us, as individuals and as a team. We just didn't know what we were capable of until we tried.

Typically, you put in 20 years and you are eligible for a pension. Now, I know none of us got paid a salary. But we will all draw a pension from MEUSA, really. You will be paid in amazing memories, pride in having participated in securing this victory and the extension of the promise of our constitution and our coun-

Complaint Department a Organization Recruiter

MOLLY MCKAY

125

try and of course an overwhelming sense of happiness knowing that because of our work, thousands and thousands of people now have access to essential protections, those 1,138 federal rights and hundreds of state rights we talked about so much. And not just that, but we helped create a cultural shift that has woven our families back into the family quilt, that gives our parents the joy of dancing at our weddings, that gives us the words "my husband" "my wife," that give our family the words "son-in-law" "my two aunts" that recognize and honor our loves in the context of our extended family.

And that is why the people in this room are more like family than friends — it has truly been an honor to serve with you my friends. I hope you choose to re-enlist in the love warrior movement and continue to serve in the cause of love and equality however your happily ever after shows up for you. I salute you, and I officially release you from this particular tour of duty. Well done, soldiers! Well done! ∞

126

Walk a Mile in My Shoes

— PETER MESH

In 1994, I fell in love with the man who legally became my husband in 2006. During the battle to have my school district recognize our marriage, I became motivated to get involved in the grassroots marriage equality movement so I took to the Internet and found Marriage Equality New York (MENY). Within a few hours of leaving a phone message, I heard back from Ron and Cathy with a resounding "YES! We'd love to have you involved!" And so it began ...

One of the MENY projects that caught my interest was the "Walk a Mile In My Shoes" campaign – a unique way for people to explain why they supported marriage equality. Each person, or couple, or family would briefly write down their story and attach their picture. Then, when we exhibited these pictures and stories, they were displayed along a pair of shoes – dress shoes, sneakers, loafers, high heels, and boots all walking in a line – now empty, but leaving their stories behind.

For over a year, our Albany chapter collected a variety of these stories and pictures.

There were stories of struggles like mine. A gay man explained that when his husband died, their marriage was not recognized by New York state. As a result, he was not only mourning the loss of his partner of 23 years, but also dealing with overwhelming estate taxes.

Stories of celebration – a young, single woman who had just experienced the joy of being the bridesmaid at her sister's wedding. Someday, she hoped to find the love of her life and get married with her family surrounding her in the same way.

Stories of support – a straight couple who were saddened by the discrimination that their gay friends faced. They wanted to be able to attend their friends' wedding just like their friends had attended theirs.

Stories of empathy – a black father and a white mother who understood the frustration of being treated differently, and wished that all loving relationships were recognized equally.

Each story was unique and powerful, and we tried to make sure that these stories were heard and understood.

Our last display was at the Capitol in Albany. Hundreds of people walked by during their lunch hour, and the shoes grabbed their attention. Many would slow down and read some stories. Some read every single story. Several stopped to have a conversation with us.

One woman, after reading several of the stories, confessed that she had never really given the issue much thought. We talked about the fact that this was true for many people, but she thought she could bring up the stories that she had seen with her circle of friends.

One man was thoroughly disgusted and worried that families with kids would walk by our display. How do we expect parents to discuss this issue with their children? We tried to explain that kids can easily understand about loving relationships … we didn't win him over, but at least there was dialogue.

Unfortunately, on that day, we left the shoes and stories for too long. While we were gathered in another location, the grounds crew came and cleaned up from the lunch crowds, and just like that, the shoes and the pictures were gone … But, they could never take our stories, and we kept telling them – in many different ways, to many different people.

In our fight for marriage equality, I believe it was our stories that made the difference. One by one, our neighbors and co-workers and state representatives would listen, and hear, and understand what it was like to walk a mile in our shoes. ∞

The Beehive Engagement

— COLLEEN MEWING

Valentine's Day was traditionally a time when members of Marriage Equality USA (MEUSA) across the United States banded together and went to their local County Clerk's office to request marriage licenses, knowing full well all same-sex couples would be turned away. We'd present the workers in the County Clerk's office with flowers and Valentine's candy. Oftentimes, people on both sides of the desk would be tearful – those asking for the marriage license and those having to tell them 'no.'

My wife and I served with MEUSA as the lead organizers in Utah for a number of years. In 2014, MEUSA Utah decided to hold two peaceful actions to celebrate Valentine's Day. We reached out to community members and selected people to be guest speakers at the Salt Lake City County Clerk's office. We also had friends perform some beautiful music. Even though Federal Judge Robert Shelby's ruling on December 20, 2013 opening the door for same-sex couples in Utah to marry, the issue was now working its way through the higher court system. Judge Shelby's window for same-sex couples in Utah to marry had closed on January 6, 2014, when the Supreme Court issued a stay on his ruling, thus stopping same-sex weddings until final disposition was reached through the appeals process. So once again, on Valentine's Day 2014, same-sex couples were turned away when they asked to fill out an application for a marriage license.

One of our dear friends, Dr. Cheryl Haws, spoke at our Valentine's Day Action that year and unexpectedly announced that she had breast cancer. This was a complete shock to us, as Cheryl had not yet disclosed this information to our community. Cheryl explained, in light of her illness, how incredi-

129

bly important it was for her to now be able to marry her wife, Shelly Eyre, so they could have all the legal benefits and protections that hetero couples did. (Thankfully, Cheryl and Shelly were able to eventually legally marry. Cheryl passed on December 3, 2015. We were all blessed and became better people as a result of having Cheryl in our lives.)

Later that same Valentine's evening in 2014, we held a MEUSA Fundraising Event at the Hotel Monaco in downtown Salt Lake City. We invited friends from all walks to include allies, family, and neighbors. The event was very successful and well-attended, raising several thousand dollars for MEUSA. In attendance were Mark Lawrence, the Director of Restore Our Humanity, who brought the marriage equality case to the forefront in Utah, as well as two of our plaintiff couples, Laurie Wood and Kody Partridge, and Moudi Sbeity and Derek Kitchen.

During the evening, we handed the microphone over to the plaintiffs so they could address the crowd. We had no idea what we were all about to witness; one of the plaintiff couples was already married, the other couple was not. However, on this magical evening, we were witness to Derek Kitchen, whom the Kitchen v. Herbert case is named after, getting down on one knee and proposing to his beloved Moudi Sbeity, placing an engagement ring on his finger. The happy plaintiff couple became engaged at our MEUSA event in front of several hundred people! Tears welled in Moudi's eyes as the two men embraced and kissed before us. Emotions soared as we witnessed this occasion together, knowing that EVERYONE in the ballroom felt the love and held no judgment. Moudi and Derek tied the knot on May 24, 2015. We attended this very public wedding, which took place outdoors with the couple surrounded by a sea of well wishers there to congratulate them.

As MEUSA Utah organizers, my wife and I were able to participate during a very special time in the historic fight for LGBTQ rights. Witnessing the proposal of one of our plaintiff couples at our MEUSA Valentine's event is definitely one of our favorite highlights, closely followed by the SCOTUS marriage ruling on 26 June 2015, which opened the door for same-sex couples to get married across all 50 states. ∞

130

My Bird's-Eye View of Kitchen v. Herbert

— JOLENE MEWING

My wife, Colleen, and I served as Marriage Equality USA lead organizers in Utah for several years. During that time, in 2014, I was able to fly to Colorado and attend one of the crucial marriage equality case hearings in person.

The week leading up to the 10th Circuit Court of Appeals hearing for the Kitchen v. Herbert case was full of excitement and anxiety. My wife and I attended a send-off rally in Salt Lake City, Utah, to show the plaintiffs the community was behind them and supported everything they had done for all of us.

Once I reached Denver, Colorado, it was time to head to a rally on the steps of the Byron White United States Courthouse, the location of the 10th Circuit Court of Appeals. The press was already there in full force, getting details and background information they could work into their stories. The weather was beautiful and perfect.

The rally was held the night prior to the case being heard in the illustrious courthouse building. The rally was put on by Why Marriage Matters Colorado. The energy level was high as a DJ cranked out music that was positive and charged. Guest speakers empowered the crowd, which grew in numbers as the evening went on.

Thursday morning, April 10, 2014, I arrived at the courthouse early to ensure myself a place inside the actual courtroom. There was an overflow room, too; however, I had been handed number 42, which guaranteed a seat inside the courtroom where history would be made.

The three judges presiding over the case, Carlos Lucero, Jerome Holmes, and Paul Kelly, loomed powerfully over the courtroom. Their many years of experience were etched on their faces. I looked at them and thought, "The fate

top–bottom

Jolene Mewing and Lawrence at the 10 Circuit Court Build Denver, CO. (2014

Jolene Mewing at "pre-hearing party the 10th Circuit Co Building in Denver (2014)

131

of marriage equality in Utah rests in their hands." I was nervous. The plaintiffs were visible sitting on a bench behind their attorneys; I could only wonder what they were feeling inside.

Peggy Tomsic commanded the room for the plaintiffs, while Gene Schaerr represented the State of Utah. They each were to speak for 30 minutes, but were allotted more time due to interruptions by the judges throughout their statements.

Besides the extreme injustice of the case itself, what made this case even more intolerable was the fact that our family's state income tax dollars were being used to pay for this case – our very own money was being used to fight against our right for marriage equality and that sickened me.

Once the hearing started, the courtroom was quiet except for those asking and answering the questions. Many times the judges spoke over the attorneys, cutting them off in mid-sentence. A few times there was a little laughter, but it was soon followed by the stark seriousness of the morning's circumstances.

I sat in silence as I watched history happening in front of me. I was there to support the plaintiffs and to be part of something bigger than I could ever imagine. When I left the courtroom, my emotions were all over the place. Murmurs started as people speculated which way the court would lean. In my heart, I knew the judges would make the right decision. I also knew that whichever way the 10th Circuit Court ruled, there would be an appeal, which meant more of our taxpayer dollars would be used to fight against my marriage.

I always felt I'd see marriage equality in my lifetime – I just didn't think it would happen as quickly as it did, or that Utah would play such a pivotal role in gaining marriage equality for all the states. After attending the hearing in Denver, I knew marriage equality was closer than it had ever been. I also knew we were on the right side of history as we watched it unfold before us. ∞

—

1 Kitchen v. Herbert https://en.wikipedia.org/wiki/Kitchen_v._Herbert

2 Opinion of the 10th Circuit Court of Appeals in Kitchen v. Herbert https://www.ca10.uscourts.gov/opinions/13/13-4178.pdf

To Have and to Hold –
Joy, Pain, and Pride on Parade

– JOY O'DONNELL

June 28, 2015 – San Francisco PRIDE Parade and Celebration

Two days after marriage equality became the law of the land nationwide, I had the once in a lifetime opportunity to celebrate a modern day civil rights victory. One I had a small but consistent role in making happen for over a decade. Very few activists live to see the wins they create, much less celebrate them. The word "epic" was made for days like this one. I was both euphoric and terrified. The depth and range of emotions swimming around inside of me were tangible and it was not even time to report to contingent line up!

As I mentally prepared myself to take my place behind the Marriage Equality USA banner with my fellow love warriors I greeted old friends and new – many of whom had become like family to me over the years. Elation filled the air and so too did celebratory bubbles and music. This created an almost other-worldly scene. I was uncharacteristically nervous and fidgeting fiercely, adjusting and readjusting my white dress and the bow on my bouquet, stickering passers-by from other contingents, creating signs, signing and gathering others to sign a rainbow flag that would be sent to the Smithsonian, posing for photos and doing interviews.

Mostly, during my frenzy of caffeine-induced activity, I was trying to fathom the profound emotional impact that the two miles and two million people that lay ahead of us on the parade route would have on me.

No skill set attained in my years of marriage equality activism could have prepared me for the flashbacks that were about to take control of my mind. Intensely painful and immensely joyful feelings and memories of events I thought I had long forgotten came back to me as crystal clear as when they

below

June 28, 2015
SF PRIDE parade –
Marriage Equality
contingent en rou
O'Donnell and Da
Kotulski.

133

occurred. The louder the cheers from the crowds lining Market Street, the sharper it all came into focus.

I've never experienced a more perfect alignment between "now" and "then."

As we began marching I remember thinking, "This is it. This is the day we worked so hard for all these years. The one we knew would happen eventually but were never sure whether it would occur within our own lifetimes. So THIS, this is what PRIDE actually means."

Since that unforgettable day, many people have asked me to explain what it felt like as I waved at the cheering masses of people lining the route. My flashbacks were memories of the motivations, the defeats, and the hope that constituted my birth as a "love warrior" a decade earlier. They came to me as a gift, as if they were on a film reel that day while on parade – playing out over and over in my head and heart. Suddenly, all at once, the years of collective love warrior work, pain, joy, heartache, loss, wins, and victory collided with my spirit and the feeling was absolutely inexpressible. To have them and to hold them from that day forward has meant everything.

This is what swirled through my mind that parade day in 2015:

January 8, 2004 – Diagnosis Day
I was diagnosed with Multiple Sclerosis, a chronic often disabling disease of the central nervous system for which there is no cure. I felt fear, I hyperventilated, and there were tears, lots of them. Life was never going to be the same. Would my dreams have to be rebuilt? I had so many more questions than answers. Uncertainty was the only certainty that day. And, how would having this disease play out in our lives without the protections offered by marriage and shared medical insurance?

February 12, 2004 – Wedding Day
Sam Carrington, my then spouse-for-life, called me at work that morning to inform me that San Francisco's Mayor Newsom had just issued the order to marry same-sex couples at City Hall. Without exchanging so much as a word we made the fierce dash to City Hall to get married. We were absolutely convinced

that if we didn't get there immediately an injunction would be filed and our window of opportunity would be gone. Super romantic, right? Anxiety about the clock, inability to "get ready" in any way in terms of clothing, hair, flowers, invites, friends, and family. None of that mattered though. That was a day we never thought would happen in our lifetime and nothing was going to stop us. We were married by then California Assemblyperson Mark Leno under the dome and in front of dozens of media cameras. We were couple number 60-something that first day of the Winter of Love. What an honor it was. We knew we were on the brink of something historic.

When they announced us "Spouses for Life" it seemed a little strange because this wasn't our first wedding. We were first married in the Shakespeare Garden in Golden Gate Park on August 19, 2001. Close to one hundred friends and family were present that day to witness our love and commitment to one another. No, it wasn't a "commitment ceremony," it was a wedding. We knew that being married in this way would make a difference in our lives and the lives of our loved ones. And, we knew that even if we could never have legal access to marriage, at least we could claim every other aspect of it.

Del Martin and Phyllis Lyon were the first couple to marry on February 12, 2004. How cosmically perfect for two women who had shared 50 years with one another while participating in decades of activism to increase the rights of LGBT people. I could not stop grinning for them and for us and for the other couples we met that day – and for the City Hall staff too – who were thrilled to be able to marry us finally after years of turning couples away. I felt joy, so much of it.

February 13–14, 2004 – Winter of Love Commences

On Friday February 13 we went to City Hall determined to serve in every way possible. We were privileged to have had the opportunity to marry on the first day and now that the media had announced it to the world hundreds of couples were about to descend on City Hall. We helped organize lines of couples, assisted in serving as witnesses, took photos, and handled misunderstandings. We provided directions and instructions. We also gave additional media interviews.

135

Valentine's Day was a Saturday and we continued to volunteer. The word about the marriages had been out for two days and the number of couples lining up to marry exploded. At one point – and so long as I live I will never forget it – I remember looking up from the bottom of the staircase under the dome and seeing dozens and dozens of weddings occurring on multiple staircases and floors at the same exact time. I saw young couples, older couples, children, families, pets, rabbis and other clergy. I saw diversity everywhere I looked, including a few heterosexual couples happy to be part of the historic day. It was a simply breathtaking, awe-inspiring visual.

Some of the couples told us that they had never dreamed of getting married because they never thought they would have the opportunity. Children were able to see their parents marry. Mothers and fathers were able to see their sons and daughters marry. Fathers were able to dance with daughters at their weddings. Terminally ill people were able to realize a dream before it was too late. These were things no one ever expected to happen. And in the months and years that followed, whenever I was feeling like I couldn't sing one more chorus of "All You Need Is Love" at a rally, or chant "Marriage Equality NOW!" at one more march, I would close my eyes and remember this day and it would all make sense again. That memory will always heal whatever might be ailing me on a given day. It was a bit like heaven as I imagine it – so much love, peace and justice.

August 12, 2004 – Null and Void Day

On the early morning of August 12, 2004, exactly six months since we married and the Winter of Love began, we stood on the steps of the California Supreme Court anxiously awaiting the fate of the 4,000 couples whose marriages would either be validated or voided that day. Standing close to fellow Love Warrior Molly McKay, as she read the ruling there was at first a burst of excitement, then a collective frown, and finally the news that indeed all the weddings had been ruled null and void. Although we had prepared for this possibility, I immediately felt numb. It felt like the weight of 4,000 couples was on our shoulders. All those people whose hopes, dreams, and hearts had been made whole again by their winter marriages.

136

We had no way of knowing the level of emotional trauma that ruling would cause – it hurt. It hurt badly. Our lives mattered. And as much as I wanted to go home and crawl back into bed and cry, I knew there was work to be done. I drank some coffee, met up with other love warriors to review our messaging and went out into the media firestorm that awaited us. Crying could come later, but directly after the ruling was issued we had to represent the thousands of couples whose lives had taken on new meaning by being married. It was time to get to work again. We all sensed that this was a game-changing moment. It absolutely disgusted me that Del Martin and Phyllis Lyon, who had been together over 50 years and who were icons of the LGBT movement, had just had their marriage declared void. Time was ticking away – would we be able to make it right in their lifetimes? We would have to at least try. There it was again, that familiar sense of urgency, no time to wait. Marriage Equality NOW.

October 11, 2004 – National Coming Out Day/ Marriage Equality Express Caravan – Washington DC

Forty-four activists crossing the United States on a tour bus, sharing with average Americans why not being able to legally marry hurt us, and our families, and America as a nation. It could happen, right? Few thought so and many warned against it. "Too much too soon," they said. They spoke as if our lives and the real ramifications of not being able to marry weren't happening in the meantime. Part of being a leader is knowing when to move forward. We knew, and we moved forward.

For those who boarded the Marriage Equality Caravan bus, our central strategy was to tell our personal stories. We refined them and shared them so that people could clearly understand what we meant to say. We described what it was like to have a partner for over 50 years and then when he passed not be able to claim his body or to bury him. We described what it was like to be denied access to shared financial assets, and then to watch his family, who had been absent for decades, show back up and claim all the money. We described how it felt to be able to legally bring a dog into the United States to live with them, but not be able to bring their life partner – effectively separating couples across national

137

borders due to not being able to marry. We described not being able to make medical decisions at times when that was needed most. We explained the privileges granted by marriage automatically for heterosexual couples.

As we crossed the nation people signed a scroll of support for marriage equality. It was addressed to then President Bush, and we laid that enormously long scroll out right in front of the White House on National Coming Out Day, October 11, 2004. It was a quiet morning – we wanted the world to see that hearts and minds were already changing.

Later that day, at a rally in front of the Capitol Building, I shared my story about being recently diagnosed with MS, the uncertainty that brought me every day, and the added strains imposed by not having my marriage legally recognized. Disclosing my MS, especially in this very public manner, was one of the hardest things I've ever done, but it was National Coming Out Day and I was committed to something much greater than myself. I knew it was the right thing to do, that my story represented many others. All our stories from the rally that day went out via C-SPAN to over 30 countries. I remember looking around at all of the caravan couples thinking that one day we would win and be proud that we were some of the first to say our rights can't wait. The year 2004 turned out to be a strong and important foundation from which I was able to launch into the next decade of marriage equality activism.

2005–2015 – Decade of Actions

This decade included wins, losses, weddings, rallies, and press conferences. We phone banked, had speaker panels, did rural outreach, and fundraising. We wrote articles and Op/Eds. We created a Loving Quilt, doing outreach to collect personal stories and photographs, and making those into quilt panels to be displayed.

I served as Marriage Equality USA's first People with Disabilities Outreach Director by organizing across the state to listen and understand how people with disabilities felt about not being able to marry. I listened to them and then reported and advocated for their concerns. (As a side note: Most of those same concerns persist today due to structural economic inequalities despite our

138

victory in obtaining marriage equality nation-wide. There is still so much more justice to be achieved!)

We participated in the Let California Ring Campaign, and we survived the trauma of Prop 8 passing. We celebrated the crushing of DOMA, the Caravan reunion in 2013, and the 10-year anniversary of the Winter of Love. And all the while we were inching closer and closer to having a marriage case, or cases, at the Supreme Court of the United States.

June 26, 2015 – Day of Decision for the SCOTUS Marriage Case Ruling

It was early morning and we were on the outside steps of San Francisco City Hall. Two years earlier DOMA had been overturned and we hoped that would be in our favor for the Supreme Court ruling on some cosmic level. This was not just another important ruling; it was THE ruling. I was feeling anxious, but also feeling confident and elated. So very many memories assailed me. My love warrior self was born in City Hall and it would be poetic to get the news that we had won right there where it all started. I was fiddling around with note cards, trying to figure out how best to say what needed to be said to the media, whether we won or lost. At some point I literally tossed the cards into the trash and instead huddled with my fellow love warriors. Several of them had been on the caravan with me and had shared in the hard work of the past years. It meant everything to be there together for each other that day. We were family.

We burst into tears when the ruling was finally released. Hugs, tears of joy, and an overwhelming feeling of "We did it!" The only sad bone in my body was the one aching for a Love Warrior we had lost along the way, our Marvin Burrows. He had so much to do with our win. I had so hoped to hug him the day we won. I lit a candle for him instead. I knew he was right there with us that day, smiling down in his angelic way at the more perfect union we had finally attained in the United States.

Full circle to the parade on June 28, 2015. These were the memories that ran over and over in my mind as I looked out at the millions of people screaming to us in gratitude. That day was one of the most meaningful, truly pride-filled days of my life. We'd said "I do" to supporting marriage equality, and we'd won! ∞

Tax Us? Then Marry Us!

— ELLEN PONTAC

The woman I used to refer to as my Partner, and with whom I had a Civil Union in Vermont, a Domestic Partnership in California, a Newsom Marriage in San Francisco in 2004, and a fully legal Marriage in California in 2008, and I joined Yolo County MECA (Marriage Equality California) as chapter leaders in 2000.

We became gay rights activists in 1981 when we successfully lobbied our City Council to pass an ordinance designed to eliminate intentional discrimination on the basis of sexual orientation. We put on the free Yolo County Gay Pride Day in Davis Central Park for 10 years, and we discovered Marriage Equality California (MECA) in 2000 when we were saying goodbye to our '50s and entering our '60s.

I realize now that, at that time, we had fully dedicated ourselves to bring marriage equality to the State of California. We did much of our work toward that goal by creating media events for our city and nearby counties. We were definitely into events! We invited everyone in our city to a Wedding Cake Cutting Ceremony and Party in Downtown Plaza when Massachusetts started offering legal marriage to same couples.

For years we went to County Clerks' offices around Freedom to Marry Day/Valentine's Day, and each time we requested a marriage license we were turned away. One year we went to three different counties. I remember that day well; it was the worst. We woke up to the news on the radio telling us that day, Valentine's Day, was the day the largest number of weddings were performed every year, and that they wished all those loving couples well. I turned to my wife and saw her crying quietly, knowing we weren't like those

ht
y. (2009)
redit: Ellen Pontac
nd Shelly, Tax Day.

redit: Sue Cockrell/
nterprise

140

"loving couples" as we would be turned away.

Being able to get married like everyone else is nothing like being able to pay your taxes like everyone else. Yet what showed me the most clearly how these events, as well as others around the state, made such a difference was our Income Tax Day event. Standing outside the post office hanging out was often pleasant. I always knew we were going to win this fight. When we joined Marriage Equality I believed that "Marriage was a Portal to Full Equality" and I still feel that way. I know that when you open the hearts and minds of every-day people they not only begin to understand what equality means, but their hearts and minds don't shut closed so easily. But I digress.

The first time we went to our local U.S. Post Office on Income Tax Day was April 15, 2004. We stood by the entry door holding our signs which said, "NO TAXATION WITH DISCRIMINATION," "TAX US? THEN MARRY US!," "2nd CLASS STATUS IS A 1st CLASS PAIN AT TAX TIME!," and our personal favorite, "NO SPECIAL RIGHTS FOR STRAIGHT PEOPLE," held by a straight person. That was back when the anti-gay folks were saying we wanted "special rights," like being able to get married.

One time someone called the police to run us off. The officer who came saw that we weren't blocking the door or doing anything illegal and promptly told the postmaster we could stay there. (The fact that she was a lesbian had nothing to do with it.) Many folks who entered the building declined to take the Marriage Equality stickers we offered. Some even made unkind remarks. I didn't let those insults get to me. I knew I wasn't alone. I had with me my old friends, as well as some I just met that day.

We returned every year for 10 years, often with families with children. We had more personal signs made by those families, and constantly adjusted our own sign which read, "TOGETHER 30 YEARS ... STILL FILING SEPARATELY." Well, that's what it said the first year. The next year 30 was crossed out to be replaced by 31, and then by 32, until finally it was impossible to read the number.

Our last year there, 2013, bore almost no resemblance to our first Tax Day event in 2004. Almost everyone, including children with their parents'

141

permission, took a sticker and smiled when we explained that they were now bound to wear it all day. Then we noticed that people were actually parking in the lot just to come to us to get a sticker to wear to show their support! I almost cried with happiness each time this happened. In fact, I'm tearing up right now as I write. My entire body is full of joy and that feeling of WE DID IT!!! It's wonderful to see the world change in your own backyard! ∞

ELLEN PONTAC

I Am Here to Inform the Nation About My Existence

— MIR REYAD

This is the day we all were waiting for. 7:30 a.m. We are here to create history. Lots of colors, balloons are around me. I see some people are very curious about the colorful get-together. The 14th of April is the first day of the Bengali calendar, "pohela boishakh." Every year we celebrate this day with a special rally, colorful Panjabi for men, saris for women. This time we have planned a rainbow rally that will move along with the "pohela boishakh" celebration rally. Everyone in the LGBTI community is excited. This is the first time we will wear Panjabi with all six colors, openly and proudly.

When we planned for this day, we created an event through Facebook. We made a plan of what to do and what not to do because we can't raise our voices about our rights, about LGBTI rights. It's illegal in our country. Even the government denies LGBTI existence in our country. But finally I am here. I am here to say, "I am a human being and I have the freedom to love." I am here to inform the nation about my existence.

We all know something can happen any time – maybe the police can come here to protest us. Maybe extremists can blast bombs or shoot us. There is panic everywhere. I am looking at everyone. Beautiful faces with smiles. Volunteers are busy giving instructions to us how the rainbow rally will enter the "pohela boishakh" celebration rally and how it will move on. I ask my friend Mamun, "What do you think?" He says, "I am thinking about marriage equality."

Suddenly someone argues, "I think it's about our existence." It's like a round-table talk show. Another one joins the conversation. He says, "I think now we should look forward, we should think about our rights, our rights to love, marriage and living like a straight person." I just listen to them. BOB

left–right

Boys of Bangladesh

Bangladesh Pride

143

(Boys of Bangladesh) and I personally believe this is the time to build up the relationship between community people and non-community people in a positive way. This is the time to sensitize our society. We love Xulhaj Mannan[1] for his energy and the way he thinks.

It's like a celebration. Everybody is hugging, laughing because it's like we have known all of them for a long time. The announcement through the Facebook event was so loud that I can see new faces from the whole country. Many straight friends of ours are here to support us. Some foreign citizens are also seen taking pictures. By this time we are hungry. Some are eating sweets, some are busy with panta-ilish, the traditional food of Bangladesh.

8:30 a.m. It is the end of all speculations: the rainbow rally starts. It looks like a beautiful, shining rainbow in the middle of thousands of colors. I am looking at everyone. Everybody is so excited. Their eyes are full of tears and shining with lots of hope. Everybody who is here is an individual hero. They are here to break the norms, the tiny mentality of society. My eyes are full of tears. I can understand it was not easy, but finally we made it. ∞

—

1 The organizer of the rainbow rally, Xulhaj Mannan, was murdered by an extremist on April 25, 2016, with another activist, Mahbub Tonoy. I want to dedicate this true event to them. May their souls rest in peace.

The Attractive Blonde Lady

— MICHAEL SABATINO & ROBERT VOORHEIS

It was an evening in the Fall of 2006 and it was our monthly Marriage Equality New York (MENY) meeting being held at the Lesbian, Gay, Bisexual and Transgender (LGBT) Center in NYC. We were in the large conference space on the first floor. There wasn't a big crowd so we set up a few tables in a square. Shortly after the meeting began, an attractive older woman with blonde hair arrived and she sat next to me. She introduced herself as Edie Windsor.

I said, "Welcome. My name is Michael Sabatino."

Her reply was, "You are THE Michael Sabatino, the marriage ambassador for Empire State Pride Agenda who handles all the blogging of the Marriage Equality news?"

I said, "Yes, that's me."

Edie said, "Thank you so much. I read all of your posts and they are so helpful and informative."

I recognized her name from the list serve and recalled that she made comments on some of the posts. I then introduced her to my husband. "Edie, meet my husband Robert Voorheis. He is one of the board members and I am the Communications Director."

Shortly after that, she leaned over to me and said, "I need help."

"What is the problem?" I asked.

She responded by stating, "My partner has multiple sclerosis (MS) and I need to get to Canada to get married as soon as possible. Her prognosis is not good and the doctor said she only has a year or two left." I conveyed my sympathies and she proceeded to supply a few more details: "My partner is confined to a wheelchair and she has very little mobility. I'm very concerned

top–bottom

Dinner with Edie
Windsor.

Edie Windsor at (
Lane Fundraiser.

below

Outside the Whit
with Edie Windso

145

about making the trip to Canada. We have been together 40 years."

I told her that we'd talk after the meeting. While the meeting was going on I became determined that I'd find a way to help this woman. Suddenly, I had a solution. I said to Robert, "How about Brendan?"

When the meeting ended I pulled her aside and informed her that we had a friend named Brendan Fay. He and Jesus Lebron founded a group called the Civil Marriage Trail. After the Canadian courts ruled in 2003 that same-sex couples there had the right to marry, Civil Marriage Trail facilitated the planning for U.S. couples wishing to travel to Canada to tie the knot.

That night, when I got home, I emailed Brendan and relayed Edie's story. Brendan got back to me and I Introduced Edie to him via email. Edie and Brendan worked on the marriage plans. Edie Windsor and Thea Spyer flew to Canada and were married on May 22, 2007 in Toronto Canada. Their Officiate was Canada's first openly gay judge, Justice Harvey Brownstone. With Edie and Thea were two best men and four best women, all of whom were assigned to a task to help with Thea and the marriage ceremony. Thea required assistance to get on and off the plane and to disassemble and reassemble her wheelchair.

Edie recalled, "I couldn't put a ring on her finger without someone holding her hand out because Thea was no longer able to lift her hand herself."

I can't help but wonder what would have happened if Edie had not come to that meeting that night and sat right next to us. Who could have predicted what the future was to hold? As the saying goes, the rest is history. What a history it is!

Edie became a member of MENY. Robert and I now feel blessed to have Edie as a great friend. As my mom used to say, "Things happen for a reason; you may not know at the time why, but at some point you will." ∞

Gus and Elmer

— MICHAEL SABATINO & ROBERT VOORHEIS

We met Gus Archilla and Elmer Lokkins in early 2004. The story of how we met is one of "something meant to be."

We were married on October 4, 2003 in Niagara Falls, Canada. About two months after we returned from Canada we came across an article in the New York Times about two gentlemen who had been together 58 years when they went to Canada to marry.[1]

Upon reading their story we decided to send them a note of congratulations. We did an Internet search to locate them and were able to send them a note which included our contact information. In our letter we suggested that the four of us get together. Shortly after that we received a phone message from Gus and Elmer stating "they knew about us." We weren't quite sure what they meant. We had been thrown out of our Catholic Church choir the week after we married and assumed that they were referring to that.[2] We called them back only to find out that they had been given a copy of the article "The New Faces of Marriage" which was written about us and which we left with the clerks who issued our marriage license. Turns out they had the same clerks. Fate is an amazing thing.

We set up a date to meet in person and we became fast friends. We talked for hours at our first encounter. We learned about their story. They met in 1945 when being openly gay was illegal. Elmer, a Veteran of WWII, was on his way to register for college. He happened to pass by Columbus Circle in Manhattan and heard Gus proselytizing. From then on they considered themselves a couple. They raised Gus's eight younger siblings. The two treasured all their nieces and nephews, often helping them with college costs.

above
Photo credit: Steven
Photography

147

Gus and Elmer

AEL SABATINO &
BERT VOORHEIS

One thing that surprised us was that they had never been to, or participated in, a gay pride parade. Well, we knew we were going to make sure they had that experience. Gus and Elmer became members of Marriage Equality New York (MENY). In June of 2004 MENY decided to ask them to be the honorees in the MENY contingent of the NYC Gay Pride Parade. At ages 88 and 85, we placed them in an open car and they experienced their first gay pride event. The reaction of the parade goers was incredible. Gus and Elmer quickly became the hit of the parade that year. The two were overwhelmed with the response they were getting from the crowd and the media. They had a very exhilarating, joyous day, a day they said "they would never forget." As the years went by, Gus and Elmer participated in several of MENY's Wedding Marches before moving to Florida to be near family members. Gus passed away at age 96 and Elmer at age 94 after being together for 68 years. ∞

—

1 http://www.nytimes.com/2003/12/16/nyregion/they-held-for-marriage-after-6-decades-decorum-public-gus-elmer-eloped.html?pagewanted=all

2 http://www.nytimes.com/2003/10/16/nyregion/bronx-catholic-parish-insists-wedded-gays-leave-choir.html

Waiting in the Gallery

— MICHAEL SABATINO & ROBERT VOORHEIS

We were no strangers to sitting and waiting for votes in the galleries of both the New York Assembly and Senate Chambers. The Assembly had already voted to support the Marriage Equality Bill on May 12, 2009. On December 1 of that same year, I received a call from Robert saying that the Senate was going to vote on the bill the next day. I was on a business trip in New England and quickly rearranged my schedule. I took a bus to Albany from Lowell, Massachusetts arriving by late morning to be present for the afternoon vote. We were uncertain of the outcome, but went into the chamber gallery with optimism. We sat there anxiously awaiting the roll call vote. The first vote cast was by Jim Alesi against; the second was by Joe Addabbo (D) — another no. We knew then we would not win this time around as both had been anticipated to vote yes. We all left Albany disappointed and determined to regroup.

Fast forward to June 2011. It was the last week of the legislative session. We arrived in Albany on Tuesday, June 21, knowing that any day now a vote would be taken on the Marriage Equality Bill. Our friends RoseAnn and George Hermann joined us as well. We had arranged to stay with our friend Suzanne Perry. However, we did not think we would be there for four days. Here was the routine: arrive to the gallery, find a seat, and wait. Once you had a seat, you stayed there except for a restroom break. We always had to make sure one of us was there to save our seats. We spent hours in that gallery day after day. We were not allowed to bring in any food or drink. After the first day of waiting we realized we needed to sneak some small snacks in our pockets. As the days wore on, more and more people joined in the gallery, many of them Marriage Equality New York (MENY) members. It became more and more difficult to

left–right

With Governor Cu

Victory in Albany.

149

leave for short periods of time and maintain our seats. We utilized whatever free time we had when the Senate was not in session to lobby some of the senators.

As the week went on, more and more people arrived from both sides of the issue and lined the halls and stairways shouting their slogans. The opposition bused people in from as far away as Texas. At one point the religious right started singing hymns in the hallways so the two of us, having sung in church choirs for decades, joined in with them. Some of the reactions we got were priceless. I think they thought all of us gays were heathens. What would we know about religious hymns?

About three years earlier, I (Michael) was traveling on business. It was a very cold morning in January. I found my seat on the plane, sat down and noticed that my wedding ring from our commitment ceremony in 1979 was not on my finger. I really panicked and called Robert to ask him to look around inside and outside the house. There was no sign of it and I didn't find it. Back to the morning of June 23, 2011, as we left Suzanne's I was getting something out of my nap sack when my bottle of vitamins opened and spilled into the bag. I reached in to gather them up, and as I did I felt something on my index finger. I pulled my hand out in total shock and disbelief. There on my finger was the ring I'd lost. As I held up my finger and showed Robert, he took it as a sign we would win and shouted, "We won!" Was the ring there the whole time? Three years later? Who knows?

Day 4, June 24, 2011, waiting in the gallery, the last day of session; it was now or never. Our state Senator, Andrea Stewart Cousins, said she wanted us to be in the gallery when the vote was taken as she wanted to refer to us when she made her statement. In the meantime the Assembly was also voting on the last bills of the session and the Marriage Equality Bill was one of them. We had two friends, Assemblymember Michael Benedetto and Assemblymember Michael Spano, who were keeping us abreast of what was happening in that chamber by text … thank God for technology. Apparently, there was some language in the bill that both chambers were trying to resolve. While the Senate met, the Assembly voted on a set of amendments developed to win the support of Senators concerned about the Act's impact on religious opposition

150

to same-sex marriage and detailed exemptions for religious and benevolent organizations. The exemptions were tied to an inseverability clause, ensuring that if the religious exemptions were successfully challenged in court, then the entire legislation and thus legal same-sex marriage would be invalid. It was becoming a long day and we were tired and hungry.

Eventually, word got out that the Assembly had voted on the bill. The time was about 9:30 p.m. The Senate voted on those amendments and it passed with little debate on a vote of 36–26. The bill itself had yet to be voted on. The Senate activity started to increase about 10 p.m. We could see that there seemed to be some dispute going on. We saw some of the senators crowded around Sen. Kevin Parker and then we saw Sen. Parker storm from the chambers. Not what we wanted to see at this stage of the evening. What we discovered was that the Republican Majority was willing to vote, but that debate on the bill was to be limited to just a few of the senators. Parker was upset he was not going to be able to speak.

Approximately a half hour later, Senator Parker came back into the chamber. We noticed many staffers were streaming into the chamber. It was standing room only. At any moment, the vote was coming. Robert had a good feeling as he had been the MENY citizen lobbyist for the last six months and had a sense from his meetings with various senators that they might have changed their opinion. Three Democratic senators who'd voted against the December 2009 bill, Shirley Huntley, Carl Kruger and Joseph Addabo, Jr. had announced earlier that month their support for the 2011 bill. On June 13, James Alesi became the first Republican senator to announce his support for the bill, and Roy McDonald announced his support one day later, thus, narrowing the requirement for passage to just one. Robert was convinced Senator Stephen Saland was going to vote yes.

Shortly after 11:00 p.m. the vote began. Senator Saland spoke from the heart and voted for the bill. Senator Andrea Stewart-Cousins never had the opportunity to speak about us. We were fine with that. The Marriage Equality Bill passed at 11:15 p.m. by a vote of 33–29. The chamber exploded into applause, cheers and tears. As order was brought to the chamber, we could hear people beginning to cheer from outside the chamber and in the stairwell in the capital building as word filtered out that "WE HAD WON!" The Governor actually came to the Senate Chamber after the vote to greet all that were there. Governor Andrew Cuomo signed the act into law at 11:55 p.m. Not wanting to spend another night away from the comforts of home, we drove home, exhausted but elated.

Marriage Equality became law in the state of New York and took effect on July 24, 2011. ∞

AEL SABATINO &
OBERT VOORHEIS

The First Marriage Recognition in New York State

– MICHAEL SABATINO & ROBERT VOORHEIS

Robert and I got married in Niagara Falls, Canada on October 4, 2003. We were unable to do it in the U.S. and we wanted to get married while my 84-year old mom (Rae Sabatino) was still alive and able to be part of the ceremony.

In 2005 I (Michael) was appointed to the Westchester County Executive Andrew Spano's LGBT advisory board. One of the many goals that the board had was to get the County Executive to issue an Executive Order recognizing same-sex marriages legally performed in other jurisdictions. He did do this in June of 2006. Since we were Westchester residents, our marriage was recognized in Westchester County. In September of that year, the Alliance Defense Fund (ADF) filed motions for a preliminary injunction and a temporary restraining order against the County Executive. ADF filed this on behalf of three residents of the county. The case is now known as Godfrey v Spano. The court of Westchester County denied the motion for a temporary restraining order.

In November 2006 Lambda Legal lawyer Alphonso David approached us to become intervener defendants in this case since we are a married couple living in Westchester. We were pleased to be asked and happy to be in for the fight. In December Lambda Legal and the County Executive independently filed motions to dismiss plaintiffs' complaints and in opposition to plaintiffs' motion for preliminary injunction. In March of 2007 we won our first major victory when the Supreme Court of Westchester County dismissed plaintiffs and denied the plaintiffs motion for preliminary injunction and ruled that the County Executive order was legally issued and consistent with New York law. The ADF decided to appeal this ruling, and in April 2007 appealed the ruling to the New York Appellate Division, Second Department.

left–right

Michael and Robe

With legal counse

Susan Sommer.

153

Well, in June 2008 we and the legal team lead by Susan Sommer from Lambda Legal and the pro bono firm of Kramer Levin lead by Jeff Trachtman headed to Brooklyn to the Second Department for oral arguments. Our team argued that Spano was adhering to New York Law which had always honored legally performed marriages from other jurisdictions. The New York Appellate issued their ruling in December of 2008 dismissing the case and confirming that Westchester County Executive Spano lawfully recognized marriages of same-sex couples. Another victory for us and the marriage equality movement.

Well, lo and behold the ADF appealed to New York's high court, the Court of Appeals. The Court of Appeals accepted the case in March of 2009. In October of 2009 we all went to Albany and Lambda Legal argued on our behalf to the state's highest court. Shortly after that in mid-November the New York Court of Appeals ruled that Westchester could lawfully extend government benefits to same-sex couples in marriages and with that, we became the first couple to have their foreign marriage officially recognized in New York State. ∞

I'll Look for Bill in Heaven and Tell Him You Are OK

— CHARLIE SCATAMACCHIA

I had a partner named Bill. We were together for 20 years. He was great. And, we were great together. We worked hard. We made a home together, a life together. We weren't totally oblivious to the outside world, but we pretty much focused on us. Then Bill got sick. He battled five bouts of cancer over 12 years before he died at age 52.

And, my life changed. I began to listen differently. To hear differently. I heard people saying, "Gays cheapen the sacred institution of marriage." And I thought, "Really? Eliot Spitzer and the prostitutes; Arnold Schwarzenegger and the maid; John Edwards and his illegitimate child; Newt Gingrich and his three wives ... and WE cheapen marriage?"
My anger at losing Bill sparked a need to do something – to help change the circumstances I now realized I had been oblivious to.

I'd previously made the acquaintance of Jo-Ann Shain and Mary Jo Kennedy – one of the plaintiff couples in Lambda Legal's marriage equality case in New York, Hernandez v. Robles. I asked them how I could get involved. Knowing I lived in Westchester, NY, they introduced me to Robert Voorheis and Michael Sabatino – two of the original founders of Marriage Equality New York (MENY).

Robert and Michael took me to my first marriage equality event – MENY's NYC fundraiser in 2010. I was overwhelmed by the energy and passion in the room.

Robert and Michael told me about an LGBTQ community center in Westchester – The Loft in White Plains. In early 2011 I attended a few meetings there and was thrilled to learn that a trip was being planned to travel to Albany to lobby New York State legislators who would soon be voting on a marriage

155

equality initiative. I boarded the bus to Albany with an amazing group of people and finally felt like I was doing something! And the effort paid off. The legislature passed marriage equality in New York State and I was hooked.

I needed to do more, but struggled to find a way to become involved. I attended the 2011 fundraiser for Marriage Equality USA on my own, determined to introduce myself to Brian Silva, MEUSA's Executive Director. Yet despite my best efforts, I failed to meet him.

However, in July, just one month later, I was finishing my volunteer shift at Roosevelt Hospital when who walked into the patient lounge? Brian Silva. He was visiting an ailing friend. I blurted out my desire to volunteer for the cause and he was lovely to me. It took some time for us to set up a meeting to discuss what I might do. In September 2011 we finally got together and talked about what I could bring to the movement.

We decided I would contribute to the MEUSA blog. That was a fiasco. Being of a certain age, I didn't have a very clear idea about what a blog was. I assumed I'd get to expound on my thoughts and ideas about all things LGBTQ – like writing op-ed pieces. Instead, what was required was reporting on the progress of various LGBT initiatives around the country. It really was much more straight-forward journalism which, I discovered, I have no talent for.

But Brian didn't give up on me. He then suggested phone banking – an integral part of the advocacy process. It was another disaster. I tried! But I just couldn't tolerate the rejection of people hanging up on me. It was demoralizing to observe the growing list of things I seemed to have no aptitude for.

Still, Brian seemed to know there was a spot for me somewhere.

I kept in touch with him and in the fall of 2012 he introduced me to Tracy Hollister, who had just joined his team. He asked me to assist her in creating "The Heart of What Matters" – a program designed to help change the hearts and minds of those opposed to marriage equality. We sought to create a forum in which people could identify significant events in their lives involving LGBT issues and craft them into compelling stories they could tell. It was very intense and meaningful work.

Then, in June 2014, Brian asked me to speak at what would turn out to be

MEUSA's last annual NYC fundraiser. (In June 2015 the United States Supreme Court effectively eliminated the need for further marriage equality fundraisers by virtue of their ruling in Obergefell v. Hodges.)

Brian asked me to do the "additional ask" for funds at that last event. I froze. I told Brian that I'd suck at that. Brian smiled and said, "Okay, don't ask for money. Just tell your story." So, here's what I said:

"When I came out to my father in 1983, he wasn't happy. But since I was single and kept a low profile, I never really gave him any reason to deal with who I was. So ... for many years we sustained an uneasy peace between us. Then I met Bill Fortune. Bill and I knew we each had found a person who would be there, no matter what ... for better or for worse, in sickness and in health, till death do us part. Though back then in New York we weren't permitted to legally take that vow, we made the promise to each other with our hearts and knew it to be true. From the beginning my brothers and their wives and my nieces and nephews loved Bill and embraced him as part of our family. But my Dad? He made up every excuse in the book to avoid meeting Bill. And, when he couldn't avoid meeting Bill any longer, the best we could ever get out of my father was – cordial. So we lived our lives. We worked hard. We bought a house together. We decorated it. We volunteered. We paid our taxes. We decorated again. We did what people do. We were a team ... Bill and Charlie. Then, when Bill was 40, he was diagnosed with the same cancer that my mother died from many years earlier. When my Dad saw how bravely Bill fought his disease, just as my mom had, and saw how fiercely I cared for Bill, just as he had cared for my mom, he finally began to understand that we were just like him. And when Bill died at the age of 52 – just about the same age my mom was when she died – my Dad was inconsolable. And just before he died at age 90, my Dad told me he would look for Bill in heaven and tell him that I was okay. Bill died before marriage equality was passed in New York State. So, even though we were together for 20 years, we never got to say 'I do.' But if you had asked my Dad at the end

of his life if he approved of my relationship with Bill, there is no doubt HE would have said, 'I do!'"

What Brian really wanted me to do was tell my father's story – which I have now told many, many times, to many different audiences at many different events. And every time I tell it, I marvel at how my father has become a posthumous advocate for LGBTQ rights.

I'm always quick to acknowledge that I came to the marriage equality movement in the final 15 minutes. But they have been a very meaningful 15 minutes to me. ∞

Testifying to Love – Why I Was Arrested

– WILL SCOTT

As an out, gay, and married priest at San Francisco's Grace Cathedral, in the spring of 2009 I was one of the lead staff persons helping to coordinate an interfaith prayer vigil on the eve of the California Supreme Court's decision on whether or not to uphold Proposition 8. At that time an invitation was extended by marriage equality activists to faith leaders and attendees from many traditions to take part in an act of civil disobedience. I, along with many others, chose to participate and were arrested the next day.

Ann Fontaine of the Episcopal Cafe encouraged me to share my reflections on what happened in 2009. I'd like to begin by thanking people for all the prayers and support they offered at the time of the action. I am so grateful for the congregants and staff of Grace Cathedral, many of whom stood alongside those of us being arrested, and those who offered their support in numerous other ways as well. At the service prior to the May 2009 march we sang a beautiful song with the refrain, "We are all in this together." The struggle continues …

I grew up in a small Episcopal Church in Virginia's Shenandoah Valley, where the tiny mid-century A-frame building on a hill and its odd mixture of congregants became for me, as a gay person, an oasis of encouragement, love, and support. When most other churches were campaigning for prayer in schools, we were learning about what we could do to end apartheid in South Africa. Other churches encouraged their flock to listen to James Dobson while we were invited to listen to the words of Archbishop Desmond Tutu. As a young acolyte there at St. Paul's on-the-Hill, I first heard about how faith compels us to stand with those pushed to the margins, and to work for justice. My civil

top–bottom

Rev. Will Scott be
arrested. (May 20

Grace Cathedral,
San Francisco.
Photo credit: bcx.ne

disobedience in 2009 was not the first time I'd been arrested while seeking to bear witness to a faith that calls us to honor the dignity of every person, and it is not likely to be my last.

How did I end up in the street? I prayed and felt inspired. On Monday night prior to our action, I was part of a group led by the Reverend Roland Stringfellow, then coordinator of the Bay Area Coalition of Welcoming Congregations, that organized an interfaith prayer vigil at Grace Cathedral on the eve of the Supreme Court's decision.

The first part of the event was filled with beautiful, moving words and music from various people of faith, while towards the end things got more explicitly personal and political. A gay couple stood up and spoke nervously for the first time of how inequality and homophobia were affecting them in the workplace, sharing how they accessed health care (one of them is disabled) and paid their taxes, but would save over $4,000 a year if they were counted the same as a straight married couple. The couple shared that they rarely came anywhere near places of worship, but this event encouraged them to speak up, even in a church. As they spoke, I thought of how my beloved Matt and I had moved from Virginia to California three years ago to be in a more supportive context for our relationship.

Next, Kip Williams, a passionate young organizer with the group One Struggle, One Fight, spoke about plans for the next day if the California Supreme Court upheld Prop 8. He then invited those in the faith community who were willing to risk arrest to stand. There was an uncomfortable pause, and a few people stood up, and I found myself standing up to join them. In some ways it was like an altar call, we were being invited to walk the walk, not just talk the talk.

At the close of the service I was asked to invite the gathered congregation to spend time praying and lighting candles throughout the cathedral. I said, "On behalf of the Bishop, clergy, and staff of Grace Cathedral I want to thank you all for coming tonight. As we move out from this sacred circle, I invite you to wander amidst the many chapels, windows, murals and icons of this holy space – a place where so many individuals, couples, and families have found solace, inspiration and strength for their journey, struggle, and work for justice. Light a candle; say a prayer for all who will be affected by tomorrow's decision. Remember that we are surrounded by a great cloud of witnesses, generations of gay, lesbian, bisexual, and transgender persons who like us struggled to find hope. As you walk past the UN mural, pray for our LGBT brothers and sisters throughout the world who share our yearning for liberation. As you walk past the icon of Mary Magdalene of the first century and Martin Luther King of the 20th remember our solidarity with women, people of color, and the poor. As you look up to the windows containing the images of scientists like Einstein and theologians like Martin Buber, remember all those who were persecuted for seeking and speaking the truth as they experienced it. This Memorial Day let us also remember the many GLBT persons who have served this country – may we discover in the courage and perseverance of all these persons reason to continue our work for justice and equality.

"And now a final blessing, The blessing of the One who liberates the oppressed, who blesses all the families of the earth, and whose name is love, be upon you and remain with you always. AMEN.

The saints who dance with us around the altar at communion, in the icons, murals, and windows of our churches to me are not static but are moving. I experience their presence as continually inviting us to make the gospel real now in our time, in our lives. We are forever invited to join them in movements for justice and equality – movements that testify to love. While the [California] Supreme Court's decision yesterday was bad news for so many, the willingness of people to stand up for the faith and hope that is within them, to testify to the love they know is real and true, is a proclamation of the good news."

The next day, on the march from the Castro neighborhood to Civic Center I was joined by an Iraq war veteran, a young Latino man named Joseph carrying an American flag and wearing his badges of honor. He was arrested as well. When I took my spot in the large circle of a 150 or more in the street outside City Hall I found myself sitting next to David, a 19-year-old transgender man who works at the grocery store in my neighborhood. When I stood up to stretch my legs I saw Brendan, a 20-something lay person from St. Gregory's of Nyssa, dancing in the circle to music provided by a visiting folk band on the sidelines. Across the circle was Rabbi Sydney Mintz from Congregation Emanu-el, a synagogue with strong ties with Grace Cathedral; Buddhist Nun Jana Drakka was sitting near Episcopal Deacons Anthony Turney and Nancy Pennecamp. Down the way from me was Reverend Dawn Roginski from St. Francis Lutheran Church, where a Morning Prayer service had prepared us for the day's work.

After we were arrested for refusing to disperse, in the paddy wagon on our way to the county jail, I learned more about Kip Williams, who said that when the day started they were praying they would have at least 30 people willing to risk arrest, but ended up with so many more. We learned how Kip's first act of civil disobedience had been at a nuclear weapons manufacturing facility in his home state of Tennessee, and how his diverse community of faith helped him in coming out. Others in the wagon talked about Paul Farmer and his work in Haiti. Each of us in some way seemed to get that what we were doing was linked to, inspired by, and related to the wider, global movements for human rights and justice.

As we were led out of the wagon and into our designated holding areas, I caught a glimpse of a young, tall African American man, whose hair standing straight up reminded me of photos I'd seen of Bayard Rustin. Rustin is someone far too easily forgotten, a gay African American man of faith who helped organize the 1963 March on Washington for Jobs and Freedom and advised the Reverend Martin Luther King Jr. on the nonviolence of Gandhi.

As I think back on our marriage equality civil disobedience in 2009, I realize that LGBT people of faith in San Francisco and throughout the world would do well to remember our connections to other movements — to gain inspiration, courage, and strength for our contemporary struggles. This is our lesson. There are many causes, and concerns worth our time and energy — may we each discern with God's help our place in the dance and testify to love. ∞

My Sordid Lives

— DEL SHORES

The year was 2008: the year President Obama was elected, the year I was legally wed in California after the state's Supreme Court struck down the ban on gay marriage.

The road to being a man living an honest gay life had been long. My dad was a Southern Baptist preacher from Texas, my mama the local high school drama teacher. I had fought back gay feelings since I could remember, and had tried to make the right choices to avoid the hell and damnation I was taught awaited me. I married a woman, had two beautiful daughters, and fought a deep, dark secret that created constant inner turmoil. Finally, after lots of therapy and purging – or perhaps embracing – some of my damage by writing "Sordid Lives" and "Southern Baptist Sissies," I was out and proud, and loudly so.

But I was still a father to two daughters. I was raising them so differently from how I grew up. When my daughter Carrie was eight, she overheard a heated phone conversation I had with my brother, a Southern Baptist minister like my father. "Why were you were fighting, Daddy?" she asked. "Because your uncle doesn't want me to be gay," I explained. She replied, "Why doesn't he want you to be gay, when you ARE gay?" From the mouths of babes! For that innocent child, it was that easy. And for her gay dad, it was a sign I was raising my daughters right, void of the bigotry that I was taught.

More signs kept appearing as the girls got older. Although we are not Catholic, Carrie and her sister Rebecca went to a Catholic high school, with mandatory religion classes. There, they couldn't help but speak out against bigotry justified by a book that also ordered parents to stone rebellious children and to buy slaves from neighboring countries. The Shores girls were

above
Del Shores and his daughters.

163

getting a reputation as shit-stirrers. Their Daddy was so proud!

When Prop 8 reared its ugly, bigoted head, now 15-year-old Carrie wanted to defend her family. She made an amazing YouTube video called "Carrie Says No To Proposition 8." She encouraged her viewing public, "Vote no on Proposition 8, for my dad, for my stepdad, for my family and for all gay people. Everyone should have the right to marry the one they love!" Proud of her message, she checked the views often and was elated that, she had gone mini-viral. Caroline Shores truly had done her part to defeat Prop 8!

On November 5, 2008, we woke up to good and bad news. The good news – we had elected Barack Hussein Obama II as the 44th President of the United States, the first African American to hold the office. The bad news – Prop 8 had passed, with only 52% of the vote, but that was enough. Gay marriage was over in California. I woke the girls up and told them the news. They both cried. Carrie sobbed. "I can't even celebrate Obama's victory, Dad, because of Prop 8. What is wrong with people?"

A week later, Carrie and I were having lunch and her mood had visibly changed. "Dad, I've been thinking about Prop 8, and it's all going to be okay!" "How so?" I asked. "They're all going to die! The haters are all going to die, Dad, and my generation will take care of this for you!" I laughed through my tears.

Carrie's optimism was dead-on. Ironically, the horrific day that saw Prop 8 passed was probably the best thing that happened to our fight for gay marriage. Our community was activated and lawsuits took our fight into the judicial system. Not since the onset of the AIDS epidemic had our community come together to fight this hard – this time, for our right to marry the person we loved, for equality.

My marriage didn't survive, but I watched the passion for equality grow in my girls. We marched together, followed and celebrated each victory. Carrie was home from college on June 26, 2015, the day of the momentous SCOTUS ruling. I woke her up the moment the news broke, and we hugged and cried and had a hard time letting go. The hug was interrupted by my phone ringing. It was Rebecca, now a school teacher, calling from across town. As a family, we celebrated together once again.

I'm very proud of my daughters. I certainly haven't been the perfect dad, but when I see their passion and their fight for their gay dad and for their family, I know I've done something right in this life. ∞

May I Have the Envelope Please ...

— BRIAN SILVA

Every door knock is an opportunity.

That is what we told every Marriage Equality USA (MEUSA) volunteer who participated in our power canvassing weekends. Truth be told, opportunities come in many shapes and sizes. Sometimes it was the opportunity for a positive signature or phone message. Other times it was the opportunity to educate and persuade. But we also had to let folks know that it can sometimes be an opportunity for rejection or even animosity.

After we won marriage in New York state and merged Marriage Equality New York with MEUSA, we began to expand our advocacy work beyond remote phone banks. One of the programs we started was our Regional Canvass, or "Power Weekends." MEUSA volunteers and their friends and family members would navigate the byzantine world of New York City's early morning subway schedules (if they were even running) on their way to Times Square. They would wander past construction and the late night club kids to make their way to our Hell's Kitchen meeting point at 5 a.m. with breakfast in hand. Depending on which state we were traveling to, a three to six-hour drive and power nap for passengers was in store.

This particular weekend we departed for Newport, Rhode Island for the opportunity to support our friends at Marriage Equality Rhode Island (MERI) in their fight for marriage equality. I always volunteered to be one of the drivers because I wanted to make the trip as easy and restful for our volunteers as possible — I already knew they would be exhausted again at the end of the day.

Newport has one of the biggest Saint Patrick's Day parades in the region and the plan was to send us there for the morning to ask residents to sign

ht

Executive
r Brian Silva and
Island Governor
Chafee celebrate
ning of the
ge bill.

ode Island
ture votes to pass
ge equality.

volunteers
uring a "power
s" weekend in
Island.

166

pro-marriage equality postcards we could mail to their elected officials. After being there from about 8:00 a.m. to 11:00 a.m., we would head up to Providence to go door-to-door canvassing. The parade was a zoo! Even at 8:00 a.m. the crowds were an immense sea of green and folks walking around with Dunkin Doughnuts cups, more than a few of which contained "homemade" Irish coffee. I wondered how the volunteers would react — an opportunity, or a nightmare?

They were fantastic! Sending folks out in pairs after a brief training, MEUSA and MERI volunteers threw all care and shyness to the wind and walked up to every shamrocked face they could find. I was particularly moved by this because I know how hard it was for some to initiate a conversation with strangers. The volunteers used the opportunity to share their personal stories of why marriage mattered to them, even to those who disagreed. And despite all the locals being there to "escape" the world and have fun at the parade, people flocked to sign our postcards. We left on a high as we drove up the state to continue our work in Providence.

When we got to Providence, we had another short training, but this one didn't go quite as well. The folks at MERI were asking us to try out a new tactic. After we knocked on a door and found a supporter, we would use our cell phones and have them leave a message with their elected official. That part we had done before. But then we were supposed to ask them if we could leave a piece of paper, have them write a personal letter to that official, then tape it to their door and we would come retrieve it in an hour.

All of us were skeptical at best, and antagonistic at worst. We knew how difficult it was just to collect signatures and to transfer someone over the phone to leave a message. Now we were supposed to ask them to write a letter in an hour and tape it outside? The entire idea of this work was to make the action as easy as possible for voters; however, this plan seemed to have the exact opposite effect.

Even as some volunteers quietly mumbled they would skip "this step," I tried to rally the troops, telling them not only could we do it, but reminding them that MEUSA was founded on believing that local communities knew best what worked for them. That meant that while we would always share our knowledge and experience, we were never going to come into their community and say "do it our way or else ..." I reminded them to think back to when others told MEUSA what we "could" or "could not" do and how that felt for us.

So with those thoughts top of mind and somewhat grudging acceptance by the volunteers, we headed out into the neighborhoods in pairs. As we started knocking on doors and talking to folks, I was pleasantly surprised that a number of people took our blank piece of paper, even if they did so while giving us a bit of a strange face. Most said "I will try," or "come back as late as you can." This went on for the rest of the day.

By the time 5:00 p.m. came around, it was time to retrace our steps, head back to headquarters to debrief, go to dinner, then off to our host families who were putting us up in their homes for the night so we could do another full day of canvassing Sunday before driving back to New York City. As I started to retrace my route, not a single paper had been taped to a door. A bit disappointed but not surprised, I decided to stop at one house where they said they would leave a letter. I knocked on the door and the woman opened it a bit flustered,

"I am so sorry!" she exclaimed. "I was just finishing the letter, can you wait a moment?" "Of course," I replied.

After she handed me the letter I was feeling really happy that someone had taken the time to write it. As I continued my walk, I was shocked to find that there were even more letters taped to doors, and a few more still inside with their owners.

When we regrouped back at the field office, the number of letters was beyond anything I could have anticipated. The volume wouldn't fill a postal truck, but each handwritten letter was a moving, beautifully written personal testament to the agony and hurt of each author on why marriage mattered to them or someone they loved. Parents writing about their children. Widows remembering lost lovers. Neighbors standing up for strangers. Each was going to be a powerful tool in our arsenal to win marriage in Rhode Island. When legislators saw that people took the time to write these (and some were an entire page long!), they would know how much people cared about and were following this issue. I was so glad that we kept our trust in our partners and put the effort into getting those letters written!

Not long after, the Rhode Island Senate and Assembly passed the marriage equality bill after some particularly harsh, bigoted and homophobic testimony from certain legislators. I think they could not believe that their colleagues, and by extension their constituents, would support this "sin." Their lashing out with such virulent language was another sign that the tide was turning and our opposition was on the defense – gasping and lashing out in anger and fear.

That afternoon, as the sun was sinking and a chill stood in the air, I stood on the steps of one of the most iconic statehouses in the nation and watched Governor Lincoln Chafee sign marriage equality into law in front of a cheering crowd of thousands. The tears of joy and jubilation at such a win, and such a public signing ceremony was written across the faces of each person there. Later that evening I was invited back into the Governor's office to take photos with our partners and present him with a MEUSA pin as a small token of our thanks for doing what was right. Our long fight was far from over, but we were one step – one state closer – to where I knew we would eventually be. ∞

May I Have the Envelope Please…

BRIAN SILVA

169

I Am No Longer That Boy

— SCOTT SMITH

When I was growing up on Long Island in the 1960s and early '70s, there were very few resources for gay people. There were virtually no role models. I didn't know anyone who was gay. Society seemed to be in denial that gays existed. The subject was not discussed in the media or in everyday conversation, except in a derogatory way – epithets intended to ridicule or bully a person. The local library had little literature with gay content, fiction or non-fiction. There were no personal computers, mobile telephones, Internet service, or other electronic means to obtain information. Aside from the lack of information, there was an official stigma attached to homosexuality. It was considered to be a psychiatric disorder, and gay sex was a criminal offense in many parts of the country. In the 1950s, an executive order was issued banning gay people from serving in the federal workforce.

In this isolating environment, I believed that I was the only person who experienced same-sex attraction. I felt terribly alone. The stigma was so strong that I was determined no one would ever know about my feelings.

Fast forward to October 11, 2009, the day of the National Equality March in Washington, D.C. I was no longer the boy who hoped no one would ever know I was gay. My boyfriend and I went to the march as members of the Marriage Equality New York ("MENY") contingent. On a bright, sunny day, hundreds of thousands of gay people, together with their friends and families, marched from the White House to the Capitol to advocate for LGBTQ equality. We wore MENY T-shirts. We carried colored MENY umbrellas. We marched past the White House chanting thunderously for equality. Indeed, I hoped the president was inside and that he could hear us.

170

When we marched past the Newseum, I read the words of the First Amendment inscribed on the front of the building: "Congress shall make no law respecting an establishment of religion … " I knew the social taboo against homosexuality stemmed from Old Testament doctrine. But Thomas Jefferson himself had stated that the First Amendment had built "a wall of separation between church and state." John F. Kennedy stated in a speech during the 1960 presidential campaign – to Protestant ministers – that he believed in an America where the separation of church and state was "absolute." The words of the First Amendment I saw inscribed on the Newseum showed how discrimination against gays violated this bedrock principle in our system of government.

At that moment in the march, standing in front of the building inscribed with the First Amendment, I began shouting "Separation of church and state!" The marchers around me joined the chant.

A blonde-haired man from the Midwest who appeared to be about 40 years old stopped me. Observing the march with members of his family, he asked me what the equality symbol stood for, and listened to me share my explanation. This man's approving smile showed me that our country had changed.

Achieving the goal of marriage equality was a stunning advancement, and the culmination of many years of struggle. It is hard to adequately express what a difference this will make in our lives and in the lives of generations to come. The gift of our struggle was not only the victorious outcome for equality under the law; it is a final liberation from damaging isolation and stigma felt by kids like the one I had been. ∞

Counter-Protesting the Opposition

— LESLIE STEWART

In early February, I believe in 2001, I was reading my local newspaper and found an article saying that Randy Thomasson of the Campaign for California Families (now the Campaign for Children and Families) would be making a stop at my own city hall, to promote keeping marriage "between a man and a woman." Marriage Equality California (MECA) had already announced a similar statewide tour for the same dates, although nothing was said about that tour in the article.

The local press conference and photo op for CCF was set for the next day, a weekday – so there was not much time to rally the troops, although I did send out emails immediately. I grabbed a couple of pieces of tagboard and made several signs, in case others could attend. The one I remember best was my personal one as a straight ally – it said, "My marriage of 40+ years isn't threatened, what's wrong with yours?"

The morning of the press conference, I made a quick stop at the nearby Safeway and bought some balloons – luckily, it was just before Valentine's Day and there were plenty of "Love" balloons available. I drove the few blocks to City Hall and waited for people to arrive. First came a car with a couple of men who pulled out a microphone, amp, etc. and began to set up on the lawn next to the City Hall entrance. Aha! Then came the press – a reporter I knew well and a television crew.

Then I walked over, with my signs and balloons, and stationed myself behind and just to the side of the speaker's spot. It was not going to be possible for the speakers to eject me without it being very clear to the press what was happening – and at the same time, any photo of the speaker would show

172

at least part of me and my sign. As it turned out, Thomasson was very civil. He introduced himself and the former state legislator accompanying him, spoke their pieces, answered a couple of questions, and left. The newspaper reporter then interviewed me and the TV cameraman got my name as well.

As I intended, both the newspaper photo and the snippet of TV news included me, my balloons and my sign, right along with the two CCF speakers. The fact that there was a counter-protester was an important part of the newspaper article as well. My sign was also quoted. Even with only one person, the protest registered. A couple of weeks later, a city councilmember congratulated me on showing up.

I signed up on Thomasson's email list to keep track of other opportunities. In 2003, CCF had another tour planned – again in February, again at the same time as a MECA tour. This time they aimed higher than the suburbs – they were going to the city of Oakland. My workplace was only a block from Oakland City Hall, so I simply brought my MECA signs to work with me and walked over to City Hall before going to the office. One other MECA protester was able to join me that cool grey morning.

Just before the scheduled time of the press conference, a woman appeared and set up a lectern and microphone and signs. Then Thomasson appeared and walked over to shake hands. He seemed a bit surprised to hear that we were there to protest and asked how I had heard about the event. I told him I had found out from his website – he seemed even more surprised that anyone would think of doing that. He returned to the lectern and we all waited. No press appeared. After 15 very quiet minutes in a light drizzle, the CCF people packed up their gear and left.

Although I still lurk on his email list, I have never seen Randy Thomasson in person again. I think that he is just as happy not to have seen me either. He is now in the position I was in at first – being interviewed because he is the only voice for the other side. ∞

Counter-Prot
the Oppositio

LESLIE STEWAR

Westboro Baptist Comes to Town

— LESLIE STEWART

In the heady days just after the California Supreme Court had ruled that marriage equality was legal, Contra Costa County was looking forward to one very special marriage. Our county clerk, Steve Weir, had said every year, when we did our marriage counter-protest, that the first marriage certificate he would issue if the law changed would be his own. Now Steve and his partner, John Hemm, were going to be married on the first day allowed in the county in the lovely park behind the county clerk's office in Martinez.

Less than two weeks before the wedding date, June 17, I scrolled through news items on my computer and came across an article about the reaction of the Westboro Baptist Church to the California ruling and upcoming marriages. Incensed that a public official would be having a headliner marriage, WBC announced they would picket the Martinez office and attempt to stop the marriage.

I spent the afternoon sending emails to everyone I could think of, starting with the list I'd built up over eight years working with marriage equality groups. We already knew that some people in our community would be coming for marriages and we had planned to have a supportive presence as much of the day as possible. Now, we needed reinforcements. I was rewarded with a flood of notes saying, "We'll do what we can — someone will be there."

I sent out directions, times, and warnings about how to handle WBC protests. On the day of the event, I came to Martinez about 7:00 a.m. — the office was due to open at 8:00 a.m., and I needed to be at work by 9:00 myself. There were already people outside the door. The Martinez police had set up some barricades which enclosed a couple of WBC protestors with signs and bullhorns

— along the sidewalk next to the street, across a small parking lot from the entrance. It looked like they were in a small cage. I spoke to everyone I could, reminding them to avoid contact with the WBC people as much as possible.

The crowd grew. Many of the newcomers told me the name of their church — I was amazed at the number of different churches. As I left for work, I met a small group in a prayer circle on the sidewalk — they had driven from Alameda, 25 miles away! As I drove past the building on my way out of town, I could hear the crowd, probably over 50 people, singing "We Shall Overcome" over the shouts from WBC, and hear the sounds of supportive car horns.

I later heard that WBC left about 10 a.m. for the "city of sin," San Francisco, and mounted an equally ineffectual protest. By that time Steve and John, with an audience swelled by some of the anti-WBC crowd, had married happily and without incident on the other side of the building. Many of those who came to show solidarity stayed much of the day to cheer the couples who came to get married. Everyone I heard from felt that the day had been a celebration — it would probably have been a much smaller event without Westboro, so in some ways we have to thank them for a most memorable day. ∞

—

http://queersunited.blogspot.com/2008/06/counter-westboro-baptist-church-anti.html

http://www.sfgate.com/news/article/Wedding-bells-still-ringing-for-gay-and-lesbian-3209166.php

Aftermath

— STEPHANIE STOLTE

It was early afternoon on the second Saturday before Election Day 2008. A particular series of events, or providence, or maybe fate, had led me to be standing in the sunshine on a small grassy knoll at the busy corner of Briggsmore and McHenry in Modesto, California. On the street corner were congregated approximately 100 folks from our community, LGBTQI and S, brave enough to publicly show their support for the NO on Prop 8 campaign. A veteran among us proudly held the Stars and Stripes aloft.

As I helped a new arrival get oriented, a man approached from the parking lot behind me with his eight-year-old daughter in tow. He stopped ten feet from me instructing his daughter to stay there and not come any closer. The girl stood with her arms akimbo and a scowl on her face as her father turned and walked in my direction. The hair stood up on the back of my neck.

Let's back up. In early July, my wife Paula and I had just started the process of becoming qualified adoptive parents in Stanislaus County and I was preparing to start a Master's Degree program in the fall. A minister who I greatly respected asked me to encourage progressive people of faith within the conservative Central Valley to support the efforts of the NO on 8 Campaign. The campaign would establish a headquarters in Modesto with trained staff and I would bring in the volunteers. As a member of the Unitarian Universalist Marriage Equality Leadership Team (MELT) and the Communities of Faith Outreach Director for Marriage Equality USA (MEUSA), it all made sense to me. I said, "Yes."

Over the summer, I gathered more and more supporters. Unfortunately, the Modesto campaign headquarters failed to materialize. However, without

my knowledge or permission, my personal cell phone number was put on the official NO on 8 website, designated as the phone number for the (non-existent) Modesto campaign headquarters. My phone began to ring again and again with calls from people who were feeling like they were under siege in their own neighborhoods, in their own homes, wondering what they could do to feel empowered. Way out of my comfort zone and not really understanding what I was getting myself into, I answered every call.

Fast forward to the small grassy knoll. It was 11 days before the election. My phone had been ringing every 15 minutes from 8 a.m. to 10 p.m. for weeks on end. I had been supporting grassroots efforts in five surrounding counties for months. I was tired and stressed out. Many of us who were visibly organizing in the Valley had received death threats. In the air, there was a feeling of escalation that threatened to lurch out of control. Privately, my goal had shifted from winning in an election to ensuring that no one was seriously injured, or worse, on my watch.

Due to the volatile nature of the marriage equality issue, our policy – at every public event – was to insist that all participants commit themselves to the principles of nonviolence. Today was no exception. As the stranger approached, I looked at him and said, "Hello." He walked past me as if I did not exist, heading toward a young man who was standing on the sidewalk, facing the street while holding a homemade sign. As he approached the young man, the stranger raised his hand in the air to reveal that he was holding something. Like a family of deer, a quiver of alarm went through the entire crowd.

Acting on reflex, I sprinted toward the menacing stranger. As I neared him, I saw that it was a Bible he wielded above his head. Now the stranger was yelling and it looked as if he intended to strike the young man with his Bible. I caught up with the stranger and did the only thing I could think of. I got right in front of him, held out my hand and said, "Hi, my name is Stephanie." I felt like a rodeo clown redirecting a charging bull. It worked. The stranger was distracted enough to turn his attention away from the young man. Then, he walked right past me once again, this time as if I was something to be avoided. He raised his Bible over his head again and loudly addressed the

177

crowd with religious condemnation.

Another wave of alarm swept through the crowd and all eyes were focused in our direction. I pursued the stranger with my hand outstretched, again saying, "Hi, my name is Stephanie." He turned away from me and walked in the other direction. A man from the crowd saw what I was doing and joined me. As the stranger walked toward him, he held out his hand and with a smile on his face said, "Hi, my name is Matthew." The stranger turned away from this gesture and back toward my outstretched hand, ping ponging between Matthew and me several times, consumed by his religious fervor.

Eventually tiring of this, the stranger brought his Bible to his side and stepped away from the sidewalk. However, he did not stop yelling. Aiming the full force of his animosity in my direction, he excoriated me for wanting to marry his eight-year-old daughter. The accusation was a sucker punch to my gut. Shocked on so many levels, I did not know how to respond. The stranger railed on as I tried to catch up with him. "I am not interested in marrying your daughter or anyone else's child. The thought of it is disgusting to me. I want to marry another adult. In fact, I already have." The stranger was so engrossed in his diatribe that he could not hear me.

A transgender woman who frequently attended our events, always well prepared for trouble, approached and trained a video camera on the stranger – the battery had been dead for two hours, but the stranger didn't know that. I have no idea what compelled me to do what I did next. I remember feeling like I was in dark territory looking for a way to de-escalate a runaway train. Stepping toward the stranger, I took off my sunglasses and said, "Can you … just for one moment … look into my eyes and see another human being?"

For the first time, the man looked right at me and for one timeless, oddly quiet moment, the stranger and I looked into each other's eyes. I have no way of knowing what the stranger saw when he looked into my eyes. But I will never forget what I saw in his. I saw blind hatred. Behind the fervor and in front of his eyes I saw a film, like a distorted lens that filtered everything he saw in a particular way. Beneath this film, I saw eyes that were free of distortion, eyes that loved his daughter deeply. I saw eyes capable of compassion. Most amaz-

178

ingly, I saw eyes that, in another place and time, could be the eyes of a friend.

As I stood there, speechless, trying to make sense of what I had just seen, the crowd felt a little more at ease, maybe even a little bit curious. The stranger seemed to shift as well. He began to talk loudly about his concern for his daughter. He was worried she would be taught things in school that were against his family's values and he did not trust his daughter's teacher to respect his wishes. A woman from the crowd stepped forward. She too was a parent of a young daughter. Guardedly, she spoke words of support to the man, telling him that he absolutely had the right to limit what his daughter learned in school.

As they talked, the man calmed down. I don't mean actual calm, more like relative calm. Like moving from 50 to 25 on a scale of 1–10. Though I never learned his name, I learned he was close to my age and had been married to his wife the same amount of time my wife and I had been together. His love for his family was clear. I also learned he was the minister of a local congregation. I looked at the man's daughter who was still standing where he had left her, arms now dropped to her sides, a look of confusion mixed with concern and curiosity on her face.

Finally, the man looked at me and said in a matter-of-fact tone, "I will never stop opposing you." I believed him, having no illusion that the scales had fallen from his eyes. However, there was less vehemence in his voice, his posture was less threatening, and no one had gotten hurt. That was good enough for me. The man turned and walked to his daughter. He took her hand and they walked away without looking back. I returned to standing watch on the small grassy knoll, somehow changed forever.

Part of me wants to leave this story right here. But I realize it might give you the wrong impression. You may believe I had managed to stop, or at least divert, the runaway train that day. In fact, I had accomplished no such thing. The train had derailed ... inside of me. Deep in my subconscious, the slumbering Kraken of my self-hatred had awakened. As I stood there trying to pull myself together, it slowly began to wend its way upward, eventually coming to rest just under the surface, outside the horizon of my conscious awareness.

There it sat, patiently waiting for me to inevitably drift into those uncharted waters. I was now destined for an epic showdown with myself in the aftermath of the campaign.

I'm not going to tell that part of my story here except to say I never did get that Master's Degree and my wife and I do not have children. We have a different life from the one we envisioned for ourselves before Prop 8. However, I can tell you what I know now that I wish I knew then ... I am the Bible-wielding preacher. I am the unsuspecting target. I am the outstretched hand, the turning away, the distorted vision, the hate speech. I am the nervous deer and the sea monster waiting off shore. I am the eight-year-old girl trying to make sense of it all. And ... I am none of it. ∞

Six Green Turtles and a Brown Giraffe

– DAVID "BEARDED IRIS" CAMERON STRACHAN

In early 2007, I read that the religious right was proposing two similar California propositions and had started to gather signatures – one defining man/male (XY) and woman/female (XX) by their sex chromosomes. I brought this to Marriage Equality USA's Christine Allen's attention when I read in the Bay Area Reporter about "marriage equality" thinking they should know about this definition effort. I "outed" myself as intersex (I have XXY sex chromosomes) and as someone involved with the Intersex Society of North America (ISNA), www.isna.org, since 1995. After a few emails discussing people with intersex variations/conditions, Christine asked me if I would consider being MEUSA's Intersex Outreach Director, which I promptly accepted. Fortunately, the "definition" proposition never went anywhere. However the other – Prop 8 – made its way into our lives instead.

By this time, Peter Tannen, and I had been loving partners for 30 years, having registered as "domestic partners" in March 1991. The previous fall, on our one-eighth century anniversary, we held a "life partnership commitment ceremony" at our favorite Sanborn Park Hostel in the hills above Saratoga. Our commitment ceremony was under a large grove of redwood trees, and Rabbi Allen Bennett officiated. When I told my mother she and my father would be getting an invitation, she kept asking, "This isn't a wedding, is it?" Well, it was "our wedding" with 40 supportive friends and my uneasy parents in attendance that first day of autumn. The ceremony was very moving, and I couldn't hold back my tears even as we exchanged our rose gold rings. We had an outdoor buffet on rustic redwood tables, fresh salads made for us by the Hostel's manager, Sylvia Carroll, played Klezmer music on our tape player, and

left–right

David and Peter, w
Andrei who they h
as he sought asyl
from Russia.

David and Peter w
full moon.

181

schmoozed on that warm first day of autumn. Having been told in 1986 that I was infected with HIV, I never thought I'd see a future wedding day. There is something very special about having others give witness to the love and commitment one shares with a beloved. But, it wasn't legal ...

On that special Valentine's Day weekend in 2004 (thanks to Mayor Newsom's wisdom), when hundreds of couples were getting married at City Hall, Peter and I were at a gay men's spiritual retreat at St. Dorothy's Rest in Occidental, CA. When we returned home we were so surprised at what was happening in our city, that Peter proposed to me hoping that we could wed on our original March 19 meeting date. I said, "Not without a diamond engagement ring!" So, we took a trip to Shreve and Company and purchased a one-third carat diamond with a band made of rose gold. Of course, I said, "Yes, I will marry you again," but the state closed down the marriages before we had a chance to sign up.

In 2007, at the LGBTI Health Summit in Philadelphia, Peter and I met Maya Scott-Chung who was displaying MEUSA's "Loving Quilt," a series of quilt panels showing queer, gay and lesbian, and mixed gendered couples. She asked us if we would like to have a panel made to represent our relationship. We said we would and when we returned home from our east coast trip, Maya and a group of students came over looking at the pictures and memorabilia that we thought would be nice on a quilt. We gave them some cloth with pictures of giraffes and a couple pictures of turtles among other items. The backstory is: on March 21 (two days after I met Peter) he sent me a card and on the front were six green turtles standing one on top of the other with the top turtle giving a branch to a tall brown giraffe to eat. Inside the card, Peter thanked me for the "nice time" we had together after we met at a bisexual potluck in Sunnyvale, CA which my girlfriend Cindy and I had advertised in the San Francisco's Bi Center's Bi-Monthly newspaper so we could meet others in the south bay. To this day, we don't know if a "Loving Quilt" panel was ever created for us even after answering a plea for a donation to help it along. One nice thing about meeting Maya was that in June 2008, she introduced and presented me with an award during the KQED-Kaiser Permanente's LGBT "Local Hero" Awards night. I was honored for my Intersex Community Volunteer Activism, and given a thick etched Plexiglas plaque on a stand. There's even a YouTube video of the event under "Intersex Elder."

So, my journey with MEUSA began. The first event I participated in was getting a ride to a Sacramento church where we were divided into groups. A few of us were sent to Antelope (just south of Roseville), to stand in front of their Walmart and ask shoppers if they supported gay and lesbian rights. It was a scary experience from all the different reactions we received. I was standing with a 23-year-old lesbian woman and I was glad to be there to protect her if any trouble arose. Fortunately, none did. Becoming the Intersex Outreach Director under the leadership of Molly McKay, I was once again hooked on educating others about the reality of intersex people. It was difficult in our "2 sex/2 gender" binary system and culture to get the organization to understand this term. Most people seemed perplexed when I mentioned that the old term was "hermaphrodite" which is what we were until doctors in the 1950s started surgically and hormonally turning us into males or females, so that our intersex nature would be erased and everything would look fine. It was done out of pure xenophobia as a "social emergency" to appease others. Many intersex people were assigned the wrong gender, have a different gender or sex identity than the two standard ones, felt shame, body dysphoria, and/or PTSD from how they were treated and very angry with what had happened to their innocent looking genitals.

I proposed to MEUSA that not all of us are "same sex or opposite sex." I often say that "Peter and I may look like the same gender but we aren't, nor are we the same sex." Most people assume their sex chromosomes are standard without ever having a karyotype performed. Some women have XY sex chromosomes (they are not transgender) but instead have androgen insensitivity syndrome (AIS), an intersex condition. They also have undescended testes (that are usually removed), blind vaginas, and cannot bear children. My variation is called Klinefelter's Syndrome. When I was diagnosed at 29 (they missed it when I was 12 years old), I was told I was sterile and that I needed to be on testosterone replacement therapy for the rest of my life since my gonads

Six Green Tur
and a
Brown Giraff

DAVID "BEARD
CAMERON STRA

183

didn't develop after my birth. I had a wild and horny puberty in my '30s. That's when I moved to San Francisco as I didn't want a long distance relationship with Peter. In January 1979, I moved my belongings from downtown Palo Alto, in my sunny yellow '65 Ford pickup truck, to an in-law apartment on 20th Street just up the hill from Noe Street. My rent was $245/month, and I had a great job at San Francisco Victoriana as their apprentice millwright.

In truth, only a few folks at MEUSA seemed interested in what I had to say about "difference." I don't know if it was fear or confusion since our system is so binaurally gendered. (Corporations make a lot of money making the genders look so different.) I maintained the Intersex Outreach webpage, held the position for three years while also being the human rights spokesperson for Organization Intersex International (OII.org). I was discouraged, and had thought that my reality could somehow help the cause. I was conflicted with the reasoning behind Prop 8 that marriage should only be between one man and one woman for the sole purpose of procreation. If this was true, what did God make me for?

Before Prop 8 passed that November, Peter and I were married in Mayor Newsom's office on the 30th of September with six friends present. We exchanged the same rose gold rings that we did 18 years earlier. That fall, we housed Jeff Girard from the Yuba City MEUSA chapter for two months while he worked as the Volunteer Coordinator at ground zero's "No On 8" headquarters on Market, the former site of Finilla's Swedish bathhouse. After Prop 8 passed, I spoke at the Join the Impact rally in Civic Center Plaza asking all bisexual, transgender, and intersex people that were legally married to come out and support us. I had Peter proudly at my side. I saw a young Hida Viloria waving to me from the crowd. (We had co-led an intersex support group years earlier for ISNA. She is now the Director for OII-USA.) I remember saying to the crowd that being a long-term HIV/AIDS survivor, I was thankful that I had lived long enough to be present as this new challenge began. It took the California Supreme Court five years to get it right, and SCOTUS another two to do the same. ∞

Keep Your Mouths Closed and Don't Look Too "Churchy"

– REV. DR. ROLAND STRINGFELLOW

Marriage is a celebration that should be shared with family and friends as the couple begins the next stage of their relationship. This is no different for same-sex couples; however, many of the current religious freedom bills and laws seek to make sure there remains a legal distinction between them and heterosexual couples. The community organizing work on marriage equality was the precursor for the Center for Lesbian and Gay Studies in Religion and Ministry's (CLGS) work in challenging harmful religious liberty laws. Rather than reinventing the wheel, we applied successful organizing strategies for this new issue. A key issue learned by the CLGS staff during the "No on Prop 8" campaign in California was that religious voices were often ignored when it came to forming the strategy to defeat this ballot measure. The "No on 8" side was determined to regain the right to marry for same-sex couples of the state. At a meeting to plan our course of action, we discovered that the strategy (including the talking points) had already been created by the political organizers. Their intention was to simply have us sign off on the plan created by the campaign "experts" they had hired. The clergy voiced concerns about these chosen talking points, which contained language that was awkward and would not resonate with people of faith on the fence with the issue. In response, we received forced smiles from the conveners that really said to us, "Keep your mouths closed! We know what is best."

Political conservatives and religious conservatives have learned to strategize together to accomplish their common goals, using fear to motivate their base in order to protect their moral cause. We saw an example of this play out in California during their 2008 Proposition 8 campaign as the Roman

185

Catholic Church and the Church of Latter Day Saints worked in tandem with political organizers. Opponents of Prop 8 (those for same-sex marriage) ran television advertisements that contained the frame of "fairness" at the core of their message (in an ad where two Mormon missionaries barge into the home of a lesbian couple, strip them of the wedding bands and proceed to rummage through their home until they find their marriage license, at which point they tear it in two). While supporters of Prop 8 (those against same-sex marriage) ran an incredibly effective ad that made parents fearful that the public schools would indoctrinate their second graders with information about gay relationships (as seen in the ad where a girl excitedly tells her mother that she learned in school how she can marry another princess when she grows up). This "fear factor" tactic to protect a particular brand of morality gets recycled over again because it is so effective in mobilizing voters.

The lesson that many on the "political left" are still learning to embrace is how to work with the "religious left" as their counterparts on the right have done so effectively. Many progressive activists are in a quandary about how to strategize when the topic of religion enters the equality conversation. It is commonplace to see a cable news network showing a left-leaning lawyer on one side providing clear and convincing arguments on why society should be more accepting of LGBTQ people. And on the other side a conservative religious leader who quotes a few passages from the Bible (as the source of their authority) and the dangers against society "going too far" will claim his position. This uneven match-up highlights that the two sides are often speaking past one another – one side speaks legalese while the other speaks for "God." It is not that the progressive lawyer does not use religious principles, but often does not have the confidence to name them as such when pitted against "The Reverend So-in-so." This is a bizarre and logically fallacious approach that many television networks take when they present two contrasting positions, as if that is sufficient to satisfy requirements of evenness and fairness – without acknowledging that it is not always the case that the two positions are equally meritorious, logical, theological, ethical, or factual. The media continues to assume that there is only one religious viewpoint on any question. They may know better, but they do not seem skilled on how to deal with religious diversity. Nevertheless, it is actually an unethical disservice for the network to present two sides as equal, which may complicate and confuse an already complex issue.

During a statewide conference call in which organizers in faith communities were planning to hold public demonstrations in major cities challenging the Proposition 8 ballot measure, each of the call participants was assigned various roles. When it was asked what the clergy could do, the response given was, "Well, you can be there. But can you not wear those things around your necks? They look too 'churchy.'" Many of us did not know if they meant our clergy collars or stoles that were too "churchy," but it made no difference because there were other organizers who had expressed their frustration over the exclusion of religious voices from our organizing. Groups like The Institute for Welcoming Resources, California Faith for Equality and The Coalition of Welcoming Congregations had begun to create an alternative path to develop strategies and talking points that were unique to people of faith, particularly Christians, who were conflicted about marriage equality. After the ballot measure did not go in our favor, efforts immediately began to repeal the new law. A new campaign was begun and we faith organizers had greater leverage to be included at the decision-making table with our faith-focused strategy. The new leadership at the helm of Marriage Equality USA recognized the importance of including faith voices and perspectives into the strategy to defeat Prop 8. We found they were incredibly open to include our unique perspective into their broader strategy.

During my tenure as the Coordinator of The Bay Area Coalition of Welcoming Congregations (the CLGS program comprising of 200+ congregations that focus on the best practices for welcoming LGBTQ people in the life and leadership of the community for the nine county Bay Area of California), we engaged clergy and laity on progressive, social justice issues such as marriage equality, health care, and creating supports for LGBTQ youth and senior citizens. But some of our most memorable work was working alongside of other marriage equality activists with MEUSA. Molly McKay, Stuart Gaffney, John Lewis and

187

others made it a point to make sure that people from a variety of religious backgrounds were included and valued. With a diverse coalition of people from Jewish, Buddhist, Christian, Hindu, Unitarian Universalist, Religious Science, and Earth Based/Indigenous traditions, the Coalition of Welcoming Congregations found that words like faith, church, even religion were not inclusive enough for our purposes. But the word "sacred" was a word that did unite us as a true coalition. Members of the Coalition also got involved to make sure there was a balance of progressive religious voices to counter conservative voices on social issues. Religious conservatives seemed to "out organize" progressives, which created the need to learn how to become more active on the front line engaging in activism. Sacred activism is the term the Coalition of Welcoming Congregations would use often to refer to the intentional action guided by prayer and meditation inspired by our spiritual conviction. Sacred activism does not have to be a "taking it to the streets/in-your-face" engagement, which happened to be the strategy we used often in the San Francisco Bay Area. It can also be non-violent, yet engaging confrontation or simply being a pacifist who believes in the power of prayer.

The most frequently asked question from clergy was, "Is there a way to motivate my members to also get involved with marriage equality efforts?" Because of the inclusiveness of the leadership at MEUSA, religious people did not need to hide their faith or be mistaken as "the enemy." An example of organizing efforts of The Coalition of Welcoming Congregations along with MEUSA was to craft a plan of action following the announcement of the Proposition 8 and Defense of Marriage Act decision by the U.S. Supreme Court. We encouraged congregational leaders to:

> *Make public statements to the media that they would still conduct weddings for same-sex couples even if the Court upheld Prop 8.*

> *Understand the theological, social, and emotional effects the court decision may have on LGBTQ people and be available to provide pastoral care to anyone needing assistance.*

188

Utilize worship liturgy that focused on the diversity of marriage and family.

Participate in the "Meet in the Middle" rally in Fresno, CA and other rallies sponsored by marriage equality activists so there would be a significant religious presence.

Clergy and marriage equality activists have come a long way in learning how to work in partnership. Many of us are grateful for the inclusive efforts on the part of MEUSA to welcome our voices and ideas to the larger strategy. These partnerships continue to this day as we organize to defeat harmful religious liberty bills and laws. ∞

Keep Your Mo
Closed and D
Look Too "Ch

REV. DR. ROLAN
STRINGFELLOW

189

Making Waves in the City of Brotherly Love

– ROBERT SULLIVAN

The symbolic and romantic idea of going to City Hall to request a marriage license on Valentine's Day was born of multi-organizational interest. Getting MEUSA involved seemed an easy task. Bill and I were excited to spearhead the local effort. As the MEUSA Regional Chapter Leaders of Philadelphia, we were full of enthusiasm and optimism about sponsoring such an event. We met with several local groups who expressed great interest in the idea. But the many voices in Philadelphia can easily drown out any single idea. Bill and I had a hard time maintaining political interest in an idea everyone personally supported. As we began planning, we could not get any participants to commit to the Valentine's Day action. Soon we faced outright resistance.

The politics of Philadelphia made it difficult for us to keep people interested in participating in a marriage equality event. People either thought the laws would change soon without their effort, or the idea was smothering other LGBT issues. I remember a minister in a same-sex marriage telling me that participation would be a conflict of interest. And the reaction to my suggestion that a lesbian couple show up in wedding gowns demonstrated a lack of real interest. Some argued that transgender rights were more important than a marriage equality action, even on Valentine's Day. And despite our efforts we could not find a trans couple in support of such an effort. Other small grass-roots organizations had an almost anti-marriage equality sentiment, fearing one issue would sell out the community. Interest in our little Valentine's Day protest was quickly fading. What started out as an awesome idea created by a coalition of local organizations became our event alone. Bill and I were feeling powerless to keep the issue alive in the media. Who were we to face the Goliath

of the establishment alone?

However, with the support of two volunteers, Tom Hall and Andy Sharpe, we decided to move ahead with the event and be the sole participants. Already being legally married meant Bill and I had to put a new twist on an old idea as we brought our marriage license from Vermont to City Hall to demand local recognition. We were in a unique situation as Pennsylvania required an identification card to vote and since Bill took my last name, his New York driver's license listed a different name than his birth certificate. Pennsylvania refused to issue him an ID, so Bill could not vote. This was a very personal issue for us. Working with our supporters, we contacted the media and noticed that while local interest was waning, national and international interest was growing. Accordingly, we intentionally made this as big a media event as possible since we were not going to have a lot of feet on the ground.

The event was a day I'll never forget. We walked into City Hall armed with our Vermont marriage license. Bill was under strict orders to be quiet and let me do the talking; after more than 20 years together, you can do that. When we got to the county clerk's office we saw dozens of members of the media. It made us nervous to walk up the long hall through the line of reporters to the clerk's door where Tom and Andy were waiting for us, holding signs. The sight of them was such a relief; we were not alone after all. The slow creep to the clerk's desk was dramatic and the media was following in our shadow, microphones hanging overhead. I imagined Bill was thinking, "What did I get myself into this time?" When we finally got there, I was prepared to give some great speech expounding the benefits to society of marriage equality. But the moment took over Bill and he began arguing "why not?" He took over the situation and I laughed, cried and died that day. It was one of those "you just wait till I get you home" moments. After leaving the clerk's office, we did get an opportunity to speak to the media and I was able to step on Bill's toes. I had to put some political logic behind Bill's emotional pleas.

Because the Associated Press picked up the story, we were invited to be on local radio and Al Jazerra where Bill managed to mug me at the microphone again. You'd think by now I'd know he's a camera hog, although in these moments I do find myself feeling proud of him for his willingness to take a stand. Al Jazerra did a large story on marriage equality with us as the featured couple. We were able to get MEUSA's Media Director Stuart Gaffney in the piece as well. In the end, we garnered more national and international media interest than we had ever anticipated, opening doors to other engagements. Soon our phone was ringing with invitations to speak on LesBe Real radio, and to be the face of marriage equality on Al Jazerra.

The event was a reminder of our wedding day. We were alone, facing the media, demanding recognition – again. This time, however, it did not end with a toast of champagne. As expected, the county clerk refused our request. As other happy couples came and went from the Marriage License Bureau, we got the bad news. "Unfortunately, at this time the State of Pennsylvania does not issue same-sex marriage licenses right now," the clerk told us. "I'm disappointed," I said, admitting I knew it was a long shot. But still, you're always surprised when you're hearing something that still doesn't make sense.

It was the strangest feeling being married, having the same last name and still being refused a local marriage license. It was a sort of legal limbo which complicated our lives in many ways. Naturally, we would get caught up in the politics of it all. And it energized us to continue the struggle for marriage equality in Pennsylvania, until May 2014 when Pennsylvania's same-sex marriage ban was ruled unconstitutional and marriage equality finally became the law of our state. ∞

People, All People Belong to Each Other

— IMAM JAMILA THARP

It was the end of 2010 and I had just recovered from a bout with cancer that year, faced with the uncertainty of whether I would stay in remission. The love of my life, my wife Michelle, and I had our then seven-year-old daughter and our two boys, who were three years old and one year old. It was at this juncture in my life that I began to take to heart the Prophet Muhammad's (PBUH) spiritual invitation to "Die before you die" which means in many Muslim traditions:

> *Live the way that you would if you had two hours to live.*
> *Live in love, live in gratitude.*
> *Tell, show, be in love.*
> *Live in Peace, live in connection.*
> *Leave nothing unsaid, undone.*

"Die before you die" is a paradoxical statement with two deaths, and a luminous life in the middle. This is what it would mean to die to your ego: Die to your selfishness. Die to the illusion that we are a perfectly self-sufficient bubble cut off and isolated, cut off from humanity, cut off from love, cut off from nature as God's masterpiece, cut off from The Source of All Being, The Reality of the Unity of the One in which we are all a part. Faced with my mortality, I found myself connected to my heart's desire for a better future for my children where humanity would understand the need to protect all people. Life is difficult enough at times. I decided to not waste time and to place my faith in the belief that together we can end the added unnecessary hardships of suffering due to discrimination. It was in this luminous light in the middle that I imagined

above

Utah MEUSA 20-y
anniversary even
Photo credit:
Jadie Jo Photography

left–right

June 2015 in Eure
at the Humboldt (
Courthouse celeb
the U.S. Supreme
decision.

June 2011 MEUSA
at Salt Lake City P
Festival.

February 2005 in
California. Unitar
Universalist mad
valentines cards
the state for Gove
Arnold Schwarze

193

what felt like the unthinkable – the idea that Utah could be the first red state to achieve marriage equality. These were my heart's whisperings when I learned I would be the intern minister for The First Unitarian Church of Salt Lake City, on the path to fulfilling my educational and professional requirements of becoming a Unitarian Universalist minister.

It was in this context that my family moved to Utah in 2011. The opportunity to learn parish ministry with the Unitarian Universalist congregation was a blessing. I joined strong social and environmental justice champions, advocating for clean air, healthy stewardship of our Mother Earth, living wages, international refugees, immigration reform, Black Lives Matter, LGBTQI civil rights and so much more. I not only found kinship and immense support in my organizing for Marriage Equality, I also found myself in the presence of many wise teachers and leaders. The opportunity to be part of the marriage equality movement in Utah was extraordinary and a wonderful experience, even if not always easy.

We arrived in Salt Lake City in the spring of 2011, just in time to rent a booth at the Salt Lake City Pride Festival in June to introduce our new Utah State Chapter of Marriage Equality USA, a cause we had been involved with since 2002. We quickly ran out of our educational materials and swag as waves of people stopped by our booth. Michelle and I took turns standing on a chair to talk to the crowd. People were overwhelmingly supportive even if somewhat in disbelief. It was obvious that people were hungry for hope. They told us their stories. They cried. They left and brought groups of people back. We collected hundreds of names and contact information. Our chapter was born. Utahns were thirsty for marriage equality. Michelle jokes that we were like John The Baptist, announcing, "Get Ready! Marriage Equality is on its way!"[1]

The first sermon I delivered as the ministerial intern at The First Unitarian Church of Salt Lake City was on why I felt it was possible to win marriage equality in Utah and in the nation with our collective engagement in "Love Warrior Work."[2] What was originally received with open arms by the progressive liberals of Salt Lake City was soon derailed by the two prominent LGBTQ Utah non-profit organizations in an infamous "bait and switch" meeting.

After my sermon, a cast of characters appeared introducing themselves as "prominent activists" for the LGBTQ community, each expressing their desire to be on my planning committee for a Valentine's Day Action in Salt Lake City. With the encouragement of my supervising minister and the church's board, I met with them.

Much to my surprise, our meeting was not focused on collaboration toward securing the over 1,400 federal and state civil rights and protections of civil marriage. Instead, it was designed to "put me in my place," to make it clear that I was an outsider and that I knew nothing about Utah. I was told that if I pursued this issue that I "would set the state of Utah back on LGBTQ civil rights issues for decades." I understood the fear expressed by those at the meeting. The LDS church actively advocated for reparative therapy, literally prescribing shock therapy as a "healing" for members whom they perceived as afflicted with the malady of homosexuality, as they called it, "same-sex attraction." Scores of LGBTQ teens were kicked out of their homes, living on the streets and committing suicide. People lost, or feared that they would lose their housing, their employment and even their children. I understood these fears. The reality is that the LDS Church's policies, in reaction to securing marriage equality nationwide, have become even more draconian in making it clear that their members who are LGBTQ, including youth, don't belong. Homelessness and suicide rates for Mormon youth have skyrocketed.

I also understood the universal truths expressed below by Rev. Howard Thurman and how these words still describe the condition for so many suffering from our country's persistent and deadly virus of racism. My family experienced the weight of homophobia with two moms and also the weight of racism directed at our middle child who is African American. These words and truth emboldened me to persevere, to keep the light of my hope and my faith kindled, but politics partly foiled my organizing for Marriage Equality as a minister our first year in Utah. I would carry Thurman's words with me to the next year following the completion of my ministerial internship when I had the opportunity to organize as a mom, a wife, and a volunteer, from a place of my full personal agency, my faith.

It becomes clear that if there are any citizens within the state who by defi-
nition, stated or implied, are denied freedom of access to the resources
of community as established within the state, such persons are assailed
at the very foundation of their sense of belonging. It reaches in to affect
what takes place even within the primary social unit, the family, where
community is first experienced. The term second-class citizen is often
used to describe such a status. This means that such persons are outsid-
ers living in the midst of insiders, required to honor the same demands of
sovereignty but denied the basic rewards of sovereignty. This collective or
communal denial of the rights and the "rites" of belonging cut deep into
the fabric of the total life of the state.

It is important to share not only what went right in my own organizing, but also what went wrong in our "Love Warrior Work" for marriage equality. I regret that the marriage equality movement lacked the imagination and courage to connect the fight for marriage equality with the struggle to secure civil rights and protections for all people. We truly need a "Rainbow" strategy and approach to ending discrimination, all discrimination. It is crucial to voice the fact that our country still struggles terribly to recognize that Black Lives Matter as well, to face our Islamophobia, both intricately interconnected phenomena and from the same ilk. My family struggled just as much due to racism and Islamophobia, if not more, than due to homophobia while living in Utah. We diligently advocated for our then five-year-old African American son to combat the intolerable racism that he endured in the Utah schools. It was a mistake on my part, and on the part of the whole marriage equality movement, that we lacked the courage, awareness and imagination to highlight the intersectionality of oppressions and to advocate publicly as strongly against racism and against Islamophobia as we did against homophobia. It is my hope that we still can.

During the fall of 2011, the state LGBTQ leadership adamantly protested the pursuit of marriage equality in Utah. At the same time, my senior minister supervisor retracted his support, as he had "worked hard to build his relationships and alliances with the state's LGBTQ leadership." It was in this context that, for the first time, my family faced a Valentine's Day without a Love Warrior action/event planned. Our then eight-year-old daughter, Abigail, was righteously indignant about our missing a year of public witness to her family's love, of doing educational outreach, of co-creating a healing opportunity to publicly challenge institutionalized discrimination on the day everyone associates with Love – Valentine's Day.

So Abigail, with her two moms' support, took charge that Valentine's Day in 2012 to ensure her voice would be heard. She created a big beautiful Valentine's Day card on which she gathered over 300 signatures from fellow classmates as well adults in her life. The Valentine was addressed to the state of Utah and was published on the front page of The Salt Lake City Tribune with an interview with her on February 14, 2012. The Valentine read:

> *Will you be my valentines Utah? My name is Abigail and I am in 3rd grade. I have 2 moms and I love them with all my heart. We moved here last year and we have no legal rights and no legal protections in the state of Utah as a family. My moms are married, but you don't recognize this. Why? Please act from Love and support my family. Family is family. Love is Love. These are my friends showing their support for my family and for Love.*[3]

As a mother, I understood that there is something incredibly damaging for a person, for a child, to be treated as though she falls outside not only that which is deemed "normal," but also outside that which is collectively held to be sacred by family, community, and even by God. One's sexual orientation, gender identity and racial identity are such integral parts of one's whole and holy self that such religiously based ostracism is not only emotionally and physically damaging, but spiritually damaging as well. Regardless of one's faith, if that faith is dictated to that person and love is withheld from her, then faith is nothing more than a jail cell that robs one's personal power, sense of self as divine and in divine connection to all that is. There is a fine line between family and public policy making. The front line of defense for family is building children's empowerment, their self-awareness and their sacred sense of connection with all that is, even in the face of oppression. Our daughter, Abby, also known by her Muslim name, Amina Nur, has known her own mind for a while now with regard to how she has wanted to express her divine light in the public realm with regard to having two moms.[4]

I eventually won over the participants in that infamous "planning meeting" by first bypassing them and organizing on an organic multi-religious faith community level, our people of faith allies for marriage equality. I remember sharing often with my wife Michelle during these months, "Just wait and see. They, (meaning the two major LGBT Utah organizations) will not want the marriage equality train to leave the station without them." Six weeks before our Valentine's Day action in 2013, I was notified that they were indeed "on board" for marriage equality and that they were willing to invest resources and money in leading Utah to secure marriage equality, as well take the lead in organizing a marriage equality "red state" coalition. Ironically, the Utah Pride Center printed t-shirts shortly thereafter, advocating for marriage equality with a picture of a train and a logo that read, "All Aboard for Marriage Equality!" I'm not kidding.

Our multi-religious coalition of support included Baptists, Lutherans, Unitarian Universalists, Mormons, Jews, Muslims, Humanists, United Church of Christ members and more. First and foremost, my goal was to engage people as educators and healers, allies from different faiths. I also built strong alliances with the mayor's office staff of both Salt Lake City and of Salt Lake County. Key to successfully awakening the divine spark of personal agency and healing with regard to marriage equality in Utah was the coming together of many faith communities and people of faith, not ceding to one narrow interpretation of faith.

I was a guest preacher and speaker at various faith communities' worship services and events as an openly out Muslim woman of faith.[5] I used Facebook to organize and get my message out. I carefully constructed a vision where I painted a picture to help everyone understand what to expect, but also so that everyone could participate in the actual co-creation of our Valentine's Day action/event.[6] For example, on our organizing web page it read:

> *What to expect? Loving faith leaders present! We will have music, song and speakers, all gathered together in the celebration of our common humanity and Love. The key points to this action are educational and healing. Each and every one of us has an immense capacity to make a difference for equality for numerous people – strangers and friends alike – by being educated and able to engage in meaningful conversations as an agent to change hearts and minds about a segment of our human family that has not been allowed to sit, to derive sustenance for fulfillment and to be seen as a family member at Humanity's table.*

When the day arrived, people were greeted by music and volunteers, lovingly dubbed "Guiding Lights" by Abigail. They held the vision of the beauty and the flow of our gathering. They greeted and provided an orientation for people as they gathered in the arboretum for speakers and singing.

Loving and committed same-sex couples peacefully requested civil marriage licenses, knowing they would be denied. The program was conceptualized as a worship service. The messaging used to organize the action was largely secular in nature, while at the same time theologically universal, focusing on the themes of love, fairness, and inclusion. Interfaith clergy fully embraced theological language in offering their support, a key contradiction to the oppressive use of religion as justification to discriminate.

The intention of this action was to be both educational and healing. We each have a part to play in changing hearts and minds about a segment of our human family that has not been allowed to sit, to derive sustenance for fulfillment, nor even allowed to be seen as a family member at Humanity's table. How do we ignite this capacity in people to be societal change agents? We take charge of the public discourse by advocating for love.

The marriage license counter action itself was a part of a larger program, sandwiched in between beautiful music, singing and powerfully spoken words shared by various community leaders and loving couples. Two dozen loving and committed same-sex couples gathered quietly, holding bouquets of flowers, accompanied by over 15 clergy members from a wide range of religious faiths. Together they ascended the stairs to the Salt Lake County Clerk's Office on the second floor. The rest of the crowd of 200 plus people stayed below. The building was well lit and open to the indoor atrium with three layers of surrounding balconies. Participants could hear beautiful music and vocals of love songs in the background.

Everyone is driven by faith, but not everyone examines their faith, re-evaluates, re-invents, and renews their faith. Yet, faith is not a dead stone. It can be the breath we take to sustain life, to move us with conscious purposefulness, sustaining us in the face of our deepest challenges and guiding us to be our best and highest self in all our engagements with humanity and with creation. And, faith can be destructive, sustaining myths of what it means to be normal defined by a narrow-minded few who possess power. And, faith can spin deeply damaging fictions of purity dividing everyone into "us" and into "them," into those who are "damned" and into those who are "saved."

The marriage equality movement in the United States of America was ignited and fueled by an awakened spirit of faith, of personal agency, for a critical mass of American people, of individuals, willing to be publicly visible, whose stories and journeys are fascinating, compelling and even heroic. Committed same-sex couples, families and children played an important role in securing civil marriage equality in Utah. An instrumental role was played by a core coalition of people of faith, including heterosexual allies, and clergy of faith in the battle for marriage equality. They brought marriage equality to Utah by not ceding the public domain to one interpretive lens of one religious faith and providing a safe and healing space for over two dozen same-sex committed couples to request civil marriage licenses on Valentine's Day. It is essential to counter the justification of using religion to discriminate against people.

I would be sorely remiss to have arrived at a time in history of having secured marriage equality in the USA to not pause and really truly think about and beyond just our achievements. I am thinking about the amazing people across our country who did the very real and hard work of tapping into their own personal agency, with a willingness to be a public "Love Warrior" for marriage equality, and I am thinking about what we might have missed.

Who did we leave out of this movement? How did we maintain structures of barriers for some groups of people to engage in the marriage equality movement? Why? How are oppressions interlocking in our lives? How might we look at how we have participated in hurting people by not inviting them into this movement or by choosing social justice language that privileges able-bodiedness like "Standing on the Side of Love," excluding those who can't stand? In many cases, though certainly not all, our successes in the marriage equality movement were achieved by mostly lesbians and gay men, mostly white, mostly middle class and mostly those who could pass for the mythical constructs of "normal." This is an essential learning needed to bring our world to wholeness and healing. Many of us are held back by our fears for good reasons. Lacking support, we particularly lack the imagination and safety to engage from our full personal power in social and environmental justice movements. My own isolation with regard to my non-binary gender identity in which my preferred pronouns are *ghe* and *ghr*, limited my full potential in my ministry and activism. I could not imagine my activism, educating, ministry and engagement with people with one more self-identification that completely fell out of the mythical idea of "respectable" western heteronormative normal.

Like many white people in our country, I have been ignorant about the pervasiveness of the disease of racism which still inflicts a great deal of harm upon our brothers, sisters, sons, and daughters who are people of color. I know I am not alone in this realization. My most difficult reflection in thinking about my work for marriage equality is a personally painful one for me as a mother. It has been painful to understand my shortcomings in perceiving, understanding and empathizing with the depth and insidious and harmful nature of racism, as well Islamophobia. People often ask me, "How was Utah for your family with two moms?" Yes, we experienced difficulties because we were a two-mommy family. Honestly though, what was far worse was the overt racist aggressions and barrage of racist micro aggressions targeted toward our

People, All Peo
Belong to
Each Other

IMAM JAMILA T

201

then four-year-old African American son. The effects of racism were detrimental to his spirit and his developing emotional and social intelligence. As an openly out LGBTQ religious leader and activist, I received death threats. I never knew the source of such disturbing threats. Did they come from an isolated person, or from within the Mormon or Muslim communities? At times, it was difficult to find solace from even within the more liberal circles of people of faith, because they unknowingly colluded with the more conservative Muslim religious clergy leaders in dismissing me as a Muslim heretic, even going so far as to ask me to cover or hide my identity as a Muslim in my liberal religious leadership and activism.

Tragically, just days ago, our country experienced in Orlando, Florida its worse mass shooting in the history of the United States of America, leaving 50 people dead and over 50 people seriously injured at the Pulse, a LGBTQ gay night club in Orlando, FL. The shooter pledged ISIS allegiance and was likely "radicalized" through the Internet. U.S. authorities describe him as a home-grown extremist who was inspired by radical Islamist groups. News reports describe him as having frequented the club regularly as a gay man. Regardless of what facts unfold, we collectively mourn for those killed, those wounded and their friends and families. As a nation, we are traumatized by this shocking massacre. As people who are LGBTQ and as people who are Muslim, we are more anxious and fearful. For those of us who are Muslim and also LGBTQ, we face a particularly complicated and interconnected set of interlocking oppressions, homophobia, Islamophobia and racism.

As a justice-seeking nation, we live in a time in which we need to not only grow our imaginations about what it means to be normal, to be a family or who it is that can get legally married, but we also need to quit ceding the public's definition of what it means to be Muslim, or to be a Mormon, to be any kind of person of faith to the fundamentalists, the extremists and the terrorists claims of what it means to be a person of that faith. Radicalized individuals and terrorist groups like ISIS and ISIL benefit by and large by the West's confusion about what it means to be a Muslim. It is important that we are not anesthetized to the very maladies that are currently killing us every day as people who are LGBTQ here in the United States, like currently still exists in Utah for LGBTQ youth.

I am a person of faith, a Muslim and a person who is LGBTQ. These go together beautifully for my family and me. Our love and our family's dedication to each other carries us through, masha'allah. Alhumdulillah, we are thriving now. This is what I want for everyone. I want us to want for each other what we want for ourselves: peace, security, protection, prosperity, closeness, meaning, connection, self-worth, equal treatment, fairness, and on and on.

Taking charge of the public discourse is key to changing hearts and minds. A profound phenomenon occurs when people's fears are met with images of Love. The simple truth that Love is Love. Family and children are natural spokespeople for Love. I think it is time to take the infrastructure we have built to gain momentum in human rights and bring our resources together to fight injustice anywhere, against anyone. Particularly we need to bear witness to the reality that Black Lives Matter, that people of color's lives matter, that first nations people's lives matter, that Muslim people's lives matter and, that a whole religion and its people are not at fault for what one unstable mind brings to bear in terror, destruction and even claims divine authority to do so.

We need to remember that "People, all people belong to each other." ∞

—

1 "Why Marriage Matters: Jamila and Michelle," http://www.whymarriagematters.org/stories

2 "Love Warrior Work" A sermon delivered at the First Unitarian Church of Salt Lake City on October 2, 2011 by Jamila Tharp, Ministerial Intern (https://youtu.be/d4QXhJxp3No and https://youtu.be/MjtmHfuwpCA).

3 "Why Marriage Matters: Jamila and Michelle," http://www.whymarriagematters.org/stories

4 More of Abigail showing up to speak her mind in the public realm: http://fox13now.com/2012/11/26/community-forum-on-restricted-book-about-lesbian-mothers/and http://www.advocate.com/commentary/2015/04/27/op-ed-12-year-old-two-moms-has-plea-all-teens

5 Examples of multi-religious faith organizing and bridge building, http://www.mttaborslc.org/pageview.aspx?id=40191, http://www.mttaborslc.org/theology-on-tap

6 http://archive.sltrib.com/article.php?id=55834101&itype=CMSID

Two Marches: the Brooklyn Bridge
and My Sunset

— DAVID THOMPSON

As I recall, the first Wedding March in 2004 began as Ron Zacchi's idea. At the time, I was co-chair of Marriage Equality New York (MENY), and Jan Thompson, the other co-chair (no relation), was away. So, I was holding down the fort. Not that I was running everything – the group was small and collaborative – but I was in charge of the meeting where the idea for the bridge march first came up. There were probably less than ten people attending that meeting at the LGBT Center, and Ron proposed a large march in support of marriage. At the time, we didn't organize big events like that – we took part in things organized by other groups, like the Gay Pride march organized every year by Heritage of Pride. We organized smaller actions, such as yearly protests at locations or events on tax day to highlight the unfairness of taxation without marriage recognition.

Ron explained that his idea was to organize a large march across the Brooklyn Bridge to rally support for marriage for same-sex couples, with the goal of attracting hundreds of participants, and well-known speakers and endorsers. My first thought was, "This is too big. We can't do it." But Ron was very excited and insistent, and I think the meeting divided about 50/50 for and against. People liked the idea, but I wasn't the only one who was concerned that we couldn't pull it off. I remember thinking to myself, "It's so easy to say 'no,' to kill an idea, but things only happen when someone says 'yes.'" So I supported the idea, and as a group we decided to explore it.

Planning the event picked up steam pretty quickly. One of the most important aspects was getting other groups to publicize it to their members, so that people would actually show up. We really didn't know for sure if we

204

were doing that successfully until the day of the march itself, but a lot of work went into it. I remember being responsible for getting the portable toilets – there were a lot of details like that which had to be taken care of. Somehow, whenever something needed to get done, someone in our group would step up and do it. Some of our wonderful long-standing members who took part were Connie Ress (at that time she was the head of Marriage Equality USA), Tim Cravens, Jim Hohl, James Loney, Cathy Marino-Thomas, Michael Ralph Sabatino, and Robert Voorheis. I know I am leaving people out – please forgive me, it has been 12 years!

To have a march, you need a permit. We did an application, and Ron and I went to a precinct somewhere in Murray Hill for a meeting. At this point, the march was just a few days away. We were shown into a room with a police captain and a couple of other officers. We sat down and the captain told us, "I am denying your application." My stomach dropped. Ron started to say something like, "You can't do this…!" He was freaking out, as was I. If we couldn't do the march, it's no exaggeration to say it would have destroyed our organization. I mustered all the calm I could and said to the captain in an even voice, "What can we do to change your mind?" And the captain calmly started talking about needing to make sure we had enough people to guide the march, and toilets – all stuff that we had, by that time, gotten totally organized. So, in about five minutes we were told it was approved. I'm convinced that we were "conditionally" approved from the beginning, and the captain told us, "No, denied." just to see what our reaction would be. If we had said, "I pay your salary, you pig!" then no permit! But we kept our cool and they saw they could deal with us.

The march itself went amazingly smoothly. Three thousand people participated, which was a perfect number. When the march crossed the Brooklyn Bridge, it looked great! And, we didn't have so many people as to overwhelm our ability to keep it organized. The weather was perfect; people had balloons and signs and t-shirts with slogans on them. A lot of local dignitaries joined us, and we got good press. I can't think of anything that went wrong.

You have to remember, in 2004, George W. Bush made the fight against gay marriage one of the centerpieces of his campaign. The officeholders that joined us were the ones that were true friends to the community, like Assembly Member Dick Gottfried from the New York State Assembly. There were still a lot of local politicians who were sympathetic but wouldn't really stand up for us. We didn't know it, but Bush's campaign turned out to be the last hurrah for our enemies in politics. Things like the 2004 march and all the ones that followed it, as well as the work done by many other groups, and the steady stream of people coming out and demanding full citizenship, swept away this opposition within a decade.

Eventually I marched "off into the sunset," and left the marriage equality movement. There were several reasons, but one of the big ones was burn out. While I was active in the marriage movement, I made it my business to keep track of what the anti-marriage people were saying and doing. I would read the websites of One Million Moms, the American Family Association, the Family Research Council, etc. The ugliness of it was pretty staggering. All three of those groups, for example, strongly opposed anti-bullying policies simply because some of the kids who would have been protected from bullying were LGBT. There was nothing these groups did that didn't come from a place of hate and lies. Exposing yourself to that is like sipping poison – little by little it eats away at you.

Late in World War II, Hitler's propaganda minister, Joseph Goebbels, made it illegal in Germany to even touch the propaganda leaflets that were being dropped by Allied airplanes over German cities. He wrote in his diary that he believed that when a person makes any contact with propaganda, it changes them. He believed that even if you are arguing against what the propaganda says, by exposing yourself to it, it changes you. So Goebbels didn't care if you were the most loyal Nazi in the world, if you touched the leaflets you had to be punished because if you touch it, it changes you. I can tell you that Goebbels was right. Exposing myself to all that anti-gay propaganda changed me. It sickened me, and I had to get away from it, and for me that meant stepping away from the marriage movement.

Thank God other people continued the fight, and that they did so with such great success! ∞

We Must Sit in the Front of the Marriage Bus

— JAN THOMPSON

The Marriage Equality New York (MENY) board I was on was a ragtag team of several middle-aged bachelors, a bachelorette, a long-term gay couple and a serial monogamist. Some of us were not necessarily marriage material, yet we all believed strongly in the right to marry the person you love, regardless of sex or gender. We believed that this one right (really a cluster of benefits) was the most important right we could get to even the playing field on a literal and symbolic level. And that was enough.

I joined MENY in the early years (circa 2000), a couple of years after Jesus Lebron had started the grassroots organization. I remember thinking one day, "Why is no one organizing around this issue?!?" only to stumble across a listing in the Center Bulletin a few weeks later. I eagerly showed up at the next meeting at the Lesbian and Gay Center (this was pre-B and T additions). I didn't have a lot of experience in activism or politics, but I knew that "the personal is political" and had the zeal and determination necessary to push past the obstacles.

In those days, marriage for same-sex couples was an idea whose time had not yet come, as we fought endlessly within our own community to educate about the importance of marriage as opposed to civil unions. The Empire State Pride Agenda (ESPA), bless them for their single issue tenacity, would not be swayed from fighting for The Gender Expression Non-Discrimination Act (GENDA), and were not yet unanimous about the decision to support marriage vs. civil union. Like the Human Rights Campaign (HRC), they felt that to ask for marriage was too much, and preferred an incremental approach to gaining marriage rights for our community. At that time, public sentiment was

left–right

Jan Thompson an⟨
Dominic Pisciotta
at MENY event.

Jan Thompson, S⟨
Jeffrey and Chris⟨
Quinn. (2003)

207

not behind us, and many in our own community saw marriage as a stodgy old institution and thought, "Who needs it?" It was not a "sexy" cause in those days, but rather a gut-felt calling for those in the trenches.

I remember a particularly contrarian lesbian friend of mine arguing against the rationale of wanting our community to participate in such a patriarchal institution. Instead, she insisted, we should work to change marriage itself to include partnership between any number of consenting adults to create a family of one's choosing (e.g. friends, aunts, siblings). While more "flexible" perhaps, I argued that the stigma surrounding same-sex relationships would not end until we had full marriage rights under the law, and to fight for an alternative would further label us as "outsiders."

As an organization we felt strongly that civil unions would set us up in a "separate but equal" situation that would be hard to overturn, and any dissenting voices in the MENY chapter quickly realized they were in the wrong organization. Our name said it all. We not only wanted to ride that marriage bus, but sit at the front of it.

In the first year I joined the organization I became its secretary, and served the next two years as co-chair. Not a lover of the limelight or public speaking, I focused my energy on organizing and rallying our grassroots volunteers. One of our biggest initiatives at the time was canvassing for signatures to support a bill to (later) be introduced into the New York senate by Assembly Member Richard Gottfried. We had on our board some smart political strategists, including my predecessors James Loney and Connie Ress. My first co-chair, Scott Jeffrey, was quite savvy in the canvassing arena, having worked for years to legalize marijuana. We were careful to ensure his pro-marijuana message did not intermingle with our own, but we needed his passion and expertise in canvassing. Scott co-led the organization with me for a year, followed by Dave Thompson (no relation), who some people hysterically thought was my husband. During my tenure other chapters started to form around the country and the national board, Marriage Equality USA (MEUSA), which had been formed in 1999, expanded and became more active. (MENY and MEUSA eventually consolidated in 2012.)

We made friends along the way with other folks like The Wedding Party who were fighting for the same thing. We butted heads with others like Evan Wolfson's Freedom to Marry, over the tactics that would work best. (In hindsight, I have no doubt some of these were battles of ego.) We were somehow seen as the fly in the ointment to their attempts to win this battle through the courts, as opposed to by legislation. In the end, what worked was coming at the issue from all angles. Pro-marriage bills introduced by the states started to turn public opinion and pave the road for the ultimate 2015 U.S. Supreme Court victory.

Those early years were a very exciting time, from rogue mayors defying their state laws and marrying same-sex couples, to the Netherlands and Canada legalizing marriage for same-sex couples for all citizens. I did not stay in the movement to the end, but proudly watched from the sidelines as it continued to grow, swell, and eventually captivate the country. It was with tears in my eyes that I traveled to the LGBT Community Center the day they announced the 2015 SCOTUS decision in our favor. I remember giving Cathy Marino-Thomas a bear hug at the press conference and participating in a celebration with thousands outside of Stonewall Inn. Thank you Edie Windsor and Brendan Fay of the The Civil Marriage Trail. Thank you Jesus Lebron and Connie Ress, the early masterminds behind much of the work. Thank you Brian Silva, Ron Zacchi and Cathy … there are just too many to name. Thanks to everyone who poured their hearts and souls into this cause! ∞

From Innocent Parent to Marriage Advocate and Activist

— SAM THORON

The story of my involvement in the movement for the freedom to marry involves more than my role on the Board of Marriage Equality USA (MEUSA). It really dates back to an evening in early 1990 when my daughter Liz, the youngest of our three children, finally cornered me and opened the conversation with the classic "Dad, I have something to tell you." "Oh, OK." She continued, "Dad, I'm gay." "Oh, OK. Are you sure?" "Yes, Dad, I'm sure." "Are you sure you are not bi?" (Somehow this would have seemed easier for Dad to accept.) "I am sure I am not bi." Then I asked what turned out to be a key question, "How do you know?" My lovely daughter looked me straight in the eye and asked, "Dad, how do you know you are heterosexual?" I got it. My orientation is just part of who I am, just as hers is part of who she is.

Shortly thereafter, my wife, Julia, and I had a tearful conversation. We ended up asking ourselves why we were so upset. Liz had not changed; we just had new information about her. We went through all the stereotypes: There won't be a wedding – well, we would support any ceremony of commitment Liz wanted. There won't be grandchildren – well, first that is her choice, not ours, and if she chose to bring up a child, either as a single mom or in a partnership, there are any number of ways to bring that about. She will get into an abusive relationship – for heaven's sake, heterosexuals invented abusive relationships. So, what were so upset about? We finally realized that we were scared. It never occurred to us that we would have a child who could be subjected to discrimination and even physical violence just because of who she is.

Julia and I quickly realized that our daughter had not changed but that we needed support to help us understand what this new information meant for

210

us and what it meant for Liz. Through a reference Liz had given us, we found PFLAG and began attending support group meetings. This was most helpful in guiding us to understanding and acceptance. In fact, my eyes were opened to my need to become an advocate by a small incident at an informal gathering after the formal support group on Mother's Day 1990. I found myself walking across the room to give my wife an affectionate hug and a kiss on the lips. It came to me that I could publicly show my affection for my chosen partner almost anytime and anyplace and no one would blink. My daughter could not. This is just plain wrong and totally unjust. I came to understand that my daughter deserves to be treated in all her affairs with the same respect and dignity which flows so naturally to her two brothers. She deserves all the rights, privileges and obligations that come with full and equal citizenship. I understood that this would not happen without advocacy on her behalf and on behalf of others like her.

Julia and I soon joined the steering committee of the San Francisco chapter of PFLAG. As the one who answered incoming calls for help, I found myself telling my story and reaching out to others. I responded to requests for public speaking and even one for a brief TV appearance. All this was new territory for me. Each time I was asked to step out of my comfort zone I had to ask myself if I cared about full equality for my daughter. The answer was, and still is, yes. I never felt I had any real choice but to step forward.

In these early days marriage seemed a very distant and secondary goal. There seemed to be too much baggage around the topic. We were concentrating on more immediate and tangible issues like housing, employment, etc. Then came Hawaii, bringing the issue to the forefront.

In 1992 I was asked to join the National Board of Directors of PFLAG as regional director for Northern California and Nevada. It was my privilege to serve on that board for the next nine years. During this period I first heard Evan Wolfson presenting his case for the importance of the recognition of marriage as a condition precedent to achieving all of the other aspects of full equality. As long as same gender unions had a status other than marriage GLBT persons would always be held as unequal, making the establishment of full

211

equality in other areas such as housing and employment more difficult and perhaps even somewhat meaningless.

It was also during this period that I first encountered our very own Molly McKay and her charm, charisma and unlimited capacity for enthusiastic action. I was hooked. My real association with MEUSA and its local presence, MECA, began. This was about the time that MECA merged into EQCA.

I remember a particular project called Know Your Allies that Molly conceived and brought to fruition. The concept was for MECA/EQCA to be the catalyst to bring together various progressive organizations up and down California so that they could know each other better should it become necessary to work together in their local communities to resist right-wing discriminatory organizations and their efforts. In about 10 days we visited some 19 communities from the Bay Area to San Diego, from the Coast to Palm Springs and north again through the Valley. The sessions were lively, beginning with Molly's version of "speed dating" as an introduction. This was followed by a more substantive discussion of challenges in the community and the resources available to meet them. Each session lasted on the order of two hours. We met many interesting folks and, hopefully, helped widen opportunities for local cooperation. As a group of activists driving together in two or three cars and having meals together, we got to know each other.

It was on this trip that Molly revealed that she was leaving EQCA. The reality is that she was pushed out the door. Because MECA had been preempted by EQCA, this led to the reactivation of MEUSA as the active Marriage Equality operating entity in California. I chose to join the Board of MEUSA, largely to provide an offset to the image of Molly's leadership as volatile, flighty, flamboyant and even attention grabbing, as it was being characterized by some in leadership elsewhere in the movement. My long record of leadership in PFLAG together with my knowledge of other local and national leaders in the movement did help increase respect for MEUSA.

I began by saying that the story of my activism and advocacy was broader than my involvement with MEUSA. My most telling "Marriage Moments" came out my appointment to the No On 8 Campaign Steering Committee as the

212

representative from PFLAG. The first of these was being asked, at the last possible moment, to write and sign the official argument against Proposition 8 in the official voter handbook to be distributed to every registered voter in the State of California. Talk about coming out and being outside of our comfort zones! Julia and I agreed. The core of that official argument is our story.

Perhaps our most exciting and challenging marriage moment was creating the first television commercial to be broadcast for the No On 8 campaign. Once again, Julia and I simply told our story and affirmed our commitment to full equality for our daughter. Making the commercial is a story in itself. It took most of the day, going over bits and pieces of the script many times with slightly different inflections and emphasis. In all there were more than 50 takes. The resulting 30-second spot proved to be the single most effective commercial in the entire No On 8 campaign.

My commitment to the marriage equality movement continued as I was invited to be a member of the Board of Directors of Freedom to Marry, Inc., Evan Wolfson's campaign for marriage equality in all 50 states.

I am proud of my contributions to the freedom to marry/marriage equality movement. It has been a challenging and fulfilling part of my life. I remain deeply committed to the principle that we all deserve to be treated with respect and dignity in every aspect of our lives, that we all deserve all the rights and obligations of full and equal citizenship in our country. Sometimes it feels like all we have to do is change the whole world. In the marriage movement, we have accomplished just that. We have changed the world.

I leave you with a final thought: The single most powerful tool we have to change hearts and minds is our personal story, our own experience, strength and hope. Perhaps this is our only really effective tool. We must always be ready to tell our story no matter how mundane and ordinary it may see to us. Tell your story. That is how we change the world, one heart, one mind at a time. ∞

Think for Yourselves. You Are the Experts!

— ANNE TISCHER

Hundreds of same-sex marriage equality activists from around the state lined the hallways of the Legislative Office Building in Albany in 2008 hoping to prompt a vote on marriage by the New York State Senate. We chanted and held up our hand-lettered signs to no avail. Although the bill had passed the State Assembly repeatedly, once again the Senate leaders had refused to take it up.

In the midst of the bedlam one woman stood out as a voice that others responded to. When word came that there would be no vote she immediately looked to ramp up pressure: " What's next?" she called out. "Shall we lie down on the floors?" Having just hosted a lawyer-advised workshop on civil disobedience in Rochester (New York) I advised her against such an action unless she had pre-planned it and knew the legal ramifications. It was a post-9/11 world and government security laws had tightened. What level of arrest might occur? What legal and financial consequences might follow, including impact on people needing clear records for future licensing as social workers and school teachers?

The woman nodded and moved to another tack. Still, she was impressive enough that I asked her name: Cathy Marino-Thomas of Marriage Equality New York (MENY).

A year later there was a vote on marriage equality by the New York Senate … that failed miserably. For decades the now-defunct Empire State Pride Agenda (ESPA) had been the large organization that directed the statewide lobbying of Albany legislators on behalf of LGBTQ rights. They had trained "Marriage Ambassadors" across the state to support their strategic plan, including me and dozens more in Western New York. Despite our unquestioning belief in

214

ESPA, we had often chaffed that we were not utilized adequately at a local level. The local ESPA organizer Todd Plank agreed and supported the "unauthorized" visibility actions in Rochester that my now-wife Bess Watts and I initiated with him under the name Social Action for Marriage Equality (SAME) and eventually Equality Rochester (EROC).

The failed 2009 marriage vote stunned everyone … ESPA had said the votes were there and we trusted them. Now we heard it could be ten years before we would see another vote. ESPA had miscalculated badly, and compounded the error by firing some of their best organizers – including Todd Plank. Rochester's circle of activists disappeared. Todd returned to activism after a short time, licking his wounds, but most other disillusioned activists were gone for good. I scheduled Equality Rochester meetings for months that no one attended – even sending out meeting minutes. It was "smoke and mirrors" but we had to keep an advocacy presence in Rochester.

Appalled at the unexpected marriage vote failure, I had immediately contacted ESPA to see what Plan B was and found there was no fall-back strategy. ESPA seemed in chaos and had no direction for us to keep momentum going. In Buffalo, Kitty Lambert, founder of OutSpoken for Equality, faced the same situation.

Kitty and I decided to drive to New York City to get direction from Cathy Marino-Thomas, President of MENY. When I asked in the large MENY meeting what we should do in Rochester, Cathy's response was life-altering: "Think for yourselves," she said, "You are the experts in Rochester." We left that meeting empowered grassroots leaders. We brought Marriage Equality New York to Western New York and it became part of the coalition under the Equality Rochester umbrella. Being a chapter of MENY gave us added credibility and confidence. And the support and guidance we got from MENY's political gurus were invaluable. They were networked throughout the state and in the halls of Albany and kept us informed.

Equality Rochester re-grouped and rebuilt after a "grassroots organizing" training guided by two of the state's most effective organizers, Rosemary Rivera of Citizen Action and Rebecca Newberry of Clean Air Coalition. Nine grassroots groups were in the room as they taught us to think strategically instead of tactically as we looked at our identified goal: to get at least one of our four local GOP State Senators to support marriage equality.

When the call came from the governor's office that grassroots organizations were invited to a "Grass Tops" meeting where we would hear the conditions that had to be met before the governor would actively promote marriage legislation, Rochester was ready. Following analysis of what led to the failed 2009 vote, the governor wanted proof that there was a strong grassroots organization in effect ... namely 1000 letters and 300 calls to each State Senator per week.

The Equality Rochester (EROC) coalition, including Rochester chapters of Marriage Equality New York, Pride at Work AFL-CIO, New York Civil Liberties Union, Metro Justice and ultimately Human Rights Campaign and Empire State Pride Agenda, led the state in terms of numbers of weekly letters and calls to our four State Senators. EROC regularly sent teams of community members to advocate at the in-district offices of our main targets GOP Senators Jim Alesi and Joe Robach. Thanks to Bess Watts and Pride at Work, the unions in Rochester were very actively contacting these Senators also. A senior staff person at Senator Alesi's office said she had never seen such intense lobbying. Finally, Senator Jim Alesi became the first Republican legislator to publicly support marriage equality ... ever ... and ignited the momentum toward final successful passage of the legislation. In Buffalo the equally intense grassroots effort spearheaded by Outspoken for Equality ultimately contributed to two GOP votes for marriage when it came to the final vote.

Looking back at the successful campaign and the vital contributions of grassroots activism, it seems clear that the five-hour trip that Kitty Lambert and I made down to NYC to visit Cathy Marino Thomas and Marriage Equality New York was fateful. The ripples of that meeting clearly influenced the outcome of the next attempt at passage of marriage equality ... and continue today. There is no going back once you have felt empowerment as an activist. Many thanks to many at MENY! ∞

Think for Yourselves. You Are the Experts!

ANNE TISCHER

Our MEUSA Family

— JOSEPH VITALE

We were a happy committed couple – **16 years** into our partnership – when a
precious little boy came into our lives. Never discriminated against, we never
felt the need to be "live" activists. Don't get us wrong: we were "check-writing
activists," but we never raised a rainbow flag in protest or support. We didn't
intentionally turn a blind-eye to the cause; it was more about never feeling the
need since we never experienced the pain of being discriminated against in
the outside world, in the office, or at home.

This all changed in January 2014, when the State of Ohio told us that our
New York marriage would not be recognized and therefore only one of our
names would appear on our son's birth certificate.

Being thrust into Henry v Hodges (which eventually was merged with
Obergefell v Hodges) was not easy. We became activists overnight, and along
with the other plaintiffs, were put into the spotlight instantaneously. We became
instant spokespeople, and others looked to us for guidance and leadership.

There wasn't an "Activist for Dummies" book available so we Googled
"Marriage Equality in the United States of America." That is when our lives
changed forever. The MEUSA connection was made thanks to the Internet.

"Hello, our names are Robert Talmas and Joseph Vitale and we are plaintiffs
in Henry v Hodges." That was the first line in an email sent to Brian Silva. The
email went on to say that we were looking to get more involved in the "cause"
and more importantly stated what we could do to help. What we didn't realize is that we were unknowingly asking Brian and the MEUSA folks for help
dealing with being pushed in the spotlight. Brian contacted us that same day
and we instantaneously became members of MEUSA.

above

Joseph, Robert, a
Cooper.

217

April 2014 – we were scheduled to appear on Fox 5 NY (our first live interview) to talk about our upcoming day in court in Ohio. We immediately contacted Brian and asked him if he could coach us on what to do and say. We even went as far as to ask him if he would come with us. Unfortunately, he was traveling. That's when we were introduced to Cathy Marino-Thomas (via email and phone). She, too, was unable to join us, but she did take the time to help coach us. Brian and Cathy's words were both comforting and precise. They reminded us what the fight was about and more importantly what was at stake. We aced the interview, and from that point on we knew that MEUSA was there for us.

Our win in April 2014 was short-lived. In November 2014, the Sixth Circuit Court of Appeals upheld as constitutional bans on marriage rights for same-sex couples in Ohio, Michigan, Kentucky and Tennessee, becoming the first federal circuit court after the Supreme Court's watershed 2013 Windsor ruling to uphold such bans and departing from recent decisions from the Fourth, Seventh, Ninth and Tenth Circuits. We were exhausted and defeated. Brian and Cathy comforted us, but the loss was a hard pill to swallow. It was at this point they reminded us that we grow from loss and disappointment and that "tomorrow is a new day."

The Supreme Court of the United States of America – how could we ever prepare ourselves for this? Don't get us wrong – we had lawyers, other plaintiffs and public relations people, but nothing gave us comfort more than our MEUSA family.

Following Oral Arguments on April 28, 2015, we walked down the endless exterior stairs at the Supreme Court of the United States of America to the waiting crowd that had gathered. In the distance we could see Brian waving us to come over. We broke away from the other plaintiffs and took the MEUSA podium. While we can't recall what we said to the crowd, we do recall looking over at Brian and seeing him with tears in his eyes. It was those tears that reminded us again what that fight was really about. It wasn't about ourselves – it was about all those who fought the fight long before us.

June 26, 2015, was an important day for the LGBT community. It was a time to celebrate, but only for a short time. Standing on the stage at The Stonewall Inn rally, we were once again reminded by Brian and Cathy that our fight was not over.

Thank you MEUSA for all you have done for the Talmas-Vitale family and more importantly our community. With your help and guidance we did our SMALL part in making history, but what we gained as humans is PRICELESS. ∞ *Our MEUSA Family*

JOSEPH VITALE

We Are No Longer Asking for Tolerance.
We Are Americans.

— JOKIE X WILSON

"We LGBTQQIs are no longer an outsider people asking for tolerance. We
are Americans. And we are not merely denizens of this earth, but citizens
of the universe in a perpetual effort to form a more perfect union with all of
its members. The theme was originally inspired by my reading of the 2008
California Supreme Court decision on marriage and the preamble to the
U.S. Constitution."

I think my statement above summarizes well what led up to my involvement
in the Marriage Equality movement. Prior to my reading of the California
Supreme Court decision in 2008, my attitude had been that I knew how I would
vote were the issue to come before me, but that it didn't feel like my issue. It
wasn't that I was lazy, but occupied with other concerns, like employment
issues and LGBT spirituality. The decision itself got me concerned and the
threat of an achieved right being taken away both frightened and infuriated
me. Of course, the promise of national success also intrigued me. It became
an issue I would fight for, not simply vote for in a distant future.

As an abstract artist, I am not cut out for portraiture. While I studied
graphic art when I was in college, that was not my calling and I did not continue
to develop my skills as per learning current computer graphics software use.
But, my conceptual art came in handy. I could suggest a theme for the 2009 SF
Pride event and that would guide the rest of the process.

At the July 2008 general membership meeting, I contributed my suggestion
for the theme. One member said it gave her goose bumps. At the September
Annual General Meeting, the SF Pride membership voted for the 2009 event
theme and my suggestion was chosen. I was later asked to provide a quote for

what inspired my theme suggestion and the result was the above quote. Others could do the graphic art, but what I said would guide it.

Beyond the art for the event itself, I was contacted by a graphic artist who was designing a window display for the Castro store, Under One Roof. I'm sorry that I do not recall his name. He was a very nice man and asked if he could use my quote as to what inspired the theme on the window display. Of course, I said yes! I asked him if he could email me the final image and he agreed. I have attached a copy for reference.

During that planning- and event-cycle and beyond, I continued to advocate for the ideas in my quote. It was time that we recognized that the U.S. Constitution did in fact, as written, validate LGBT rights and marriage equality. As more states adopted marriage equality as policy, I used social media to share articles that covered the progress of the movement. I read many more than I shared, because I wanted to make understanding of the legal and political issues as easy as possible for anyone who was trying to follow the movement through my postings. Friends repeatedly thanked me for this, so I felt obligated to keep it going until the final victories with the SCOTUS, first with the Prop 8 issue and then the final cases that made same-sex marriage legal nationally.

As part of my own education, I eventually read the decisions from all of the first few states to adopt marriage equality. Those included Massachusetts, Connecticut, and Iowa. (I had already read the California decision.) I also read the brief Hawaii decision in order to understand what happened there. I also read the Walker decision about Prop 8 in California and the Ninth Circuit appeal decision, my favorite, since it had funny jokes in it. I largely stopped there, as remaining decisions largely reiterated what had been stated in the decisions I had already read. As we got well into the issue, with many states having adopted marriage equality as policy, I joked that all that was left was for the judges to get in a memorable quote, which a few managed.

In 2013, at a San Francisco Pride general membership meeting, a board member, Justin Taylor, announced that security volunteers were needed for the Day of Decision protest or celebration (not knowing the decision yet, we were not sure which it would be) in the Castro. Having a paternal sense of

We Are No Lor
Asking for
Tolerance. We
Are American

JOKIE X WILSON

221

protecting my community, I decided to forgo the partying and volunteer to help keep my community safe. The celebration turned out to have no major problems. A little girl with her mom gave me an HRC = flag, which I still keep on my desk at home.

In 2015, I volunteered again to do security at that year's Day of Decision party. Even as the issue was bigger, involving a decision for the Supreme Court of the United States, the crowd that gathered was half the size of that for the Prop 8 decision. That gave me a little more freedom, so I took advantage of that to dance on the stage at the end of the event.

Throughout all of this, I used mail art to keep friends around the world informed about what was going on. I made postcards out of SF Pride imagery as well as some small posters. Being a big ham, I soaked up the attention I got for my theme suggestion and additional quote. But I didn't simply enjoy the attention. That's never enough for me. I wanted to plant seeds, inspire others. I didn't want a pedestal. I wanted to generate ideas, enliven those burnt out from years of struggle. I wanted to get others to believe they could be successful with LGBT rights as well. And I wanted members of my community to feel dignified, validated, and important.

As a funny aside, I kept so informed about the issues as they unfolded and was so able to consistently answer questions, probably with more detail than necessary, that likely contributed to my reputation for being rather verbose. When I mentioned to friends that I had traveled to Ireland and kissed the Blarney Stone, which is supposed to then provide the gift of eloquence, friends teased me that I probably recharged it. ∞

We Are No nger Asking for Tolerance. We re Americans.

JOKIE X WILSON

I'm 77 Years Old and I Can't Wait!

— EDIE WINDSOR

On May 22, 2007, Thea Spyer and I were legally married in Toronto, Canada. When we returned to New York, we were anxious to find a way to have our marriage recognized in our home state.

Later that year, Thea and I attended a town hall meeting at the LGBT Center in New York City that had been organized by Marriage Equality New York (MENY). They were planning to have a variety of speakers to talk about the upcoming elections, the New York State Senate and other issues concerning our community. That was a very special night. I arrived, pushing Thea in her wheelchair, and the room was very big and there were just a few people. Suddenly, though, it was mobbed! I needed help finding a seat, so I approached a woman who seemed in charge and told her I needed a spot in the front for my wife's wheelchair, telling her we can't sit in back. She was very helpful and brought us to the front. I later learned she was the head of MENY, Cathy Marino-Thomas, who later became a very dear friend.

That night there was someone there from HRC who was bringing us up-to-date on how the world was. And he was saying, "We are just in line with the administration, we have exactly the same agenda, and our timing is the same," and he named all the things. Then someone in the audience said, "What about marriage?" And he said arrogantly, "Well that's a couple years down the pike." His tone implied "marriage is not of interest now in our incredibly wonderful and highly respected agenda."

I couldn't believe what he said, or how he was saying it! So I raised my hand and I was a little surprised when Cathy came down from the stage with the microphone and stuck it in my mouth. I said, "I'm 77 years old and I can't

223

wait!! What do we have to do?" On that same night I signed up as a Marriage Ambassador.

From then on Thea and I were at every MENY rally, speech and public event we could attend, given Thea's condition. After Thea died and I won my case at the Supreme Court, I continued to support (now) MEUSA, attending and speaking at events and rallies because even though I won, we still didn't have full marriage equality in the U.S. ∞

Freedom to Marry – the Journey to Justice

— LAURIE YORK & CARMEN GOODYEAR

After morning farm chores of milking the goats and feeding the chickens here on our small farm in Northern California, we got an email from our friends in New York. "Phyl and Del were just married in San Francisco!" We gathered our camera equipment and arranged for farm care, jumped in the truck, and headed to San Francisco. Hours later, we found ourselves on the steps of City Hall. We filmed angry protesters on the stairs waving signs – "God Hates Fags!" – while crowds of happy, same-sex couples passed by, entering the rotunda of love.

Once inside, as we interviewed beaming, loving couples waiting in line for a marriage license, we were overcome by the magnitude of this historical event. Mayor Newsom had opened the doors to these 4,000 couples and said, "Come on in – join the rest of us!" The public acceptance was something many of these couples, including ourselves, were experiencing for the first time in our lives.

The line of couples waiting to get a license snaked through the government halls, and it was a slow shuffle to get to the Recorder's Office. We immediately made friends with Don Williams and David Jones, who were standing in front of us. They had been together for 24 years, but now they were anxious to tie the knot legally. They were afraid that if they didn't get their license that day, the opportunity might be shut down. They educated us on the history of civil rights struggles and agreed to be interviewed for the film that was percolating in our minds. Behind us in line were Diana Berry and Karla Kyrias, a young couple thrilled to start their lives together with a legitimate marriage. The six of us became witnesses for each other's ceremonies and gave hugs and kisses all around.

below

Laurie and Carme

225